52 Toys & Puzzles for the Weekend Woodworker

John A. Nelson

STERLING PUBLISHING CO., INC. NEW YORK

Dedication

To my lifelong friend Edgar Edwards, who just became a grandfather. I'm sure he will want to make at least one of each of these 52 projects for his granddaughter.

Acknowledgments

I wish to thank Deborah Porter Hayes for taking all the photographs of the projects; they are just great.

I extend my thanks to John Woodside, editorial director, Rodman Neumann, editor, and the staff at STERLING PUBLISHING CO., who transformed my manuscript and art into this book.

I especially want to thank my wife, Joyce, for typing my scribbling into a readable manuscript; my daughter, Jennifer, for helping paint some of the projects; my two grandchildren, Hilary and Daniel O'Rourke, who were my mentors in doing this book; Mr. and Mrs. Fred Fosher for letting me copy their "book house"; Mr. Fred Miller for letting me copy his Mexican child's chair; local antique dealer Marny Bean for letting me copy the alligator and eating chickens, circa 1880, projects; and the many long-forgotten fathers and grandfathers who made the original projects in my section of the toys from yesterday.

To the woodworkers who make these projects and to the children who play with them, I hope you like and enjoy them.

Library of Congress Cataloging-in-Publication Data

Nelson, John A., 1935–
    52 toys & puzzles for the weekend woodworker / John A. Nelson.
        p. cm.
    Includes index.
    ISBN 0-8069-0644-8
    1. Wooden toy making. 2. Puzzles. I. Title. II. Title: Fifty-two toys and puzzles for the weekend woodworker.
TT174.5.W6N45 1994
745.592—dc20   94-2372
                                                            CIP

Edited by R. P. Neumann

10 9 8 7 6 5 4 3 2 1

Published by Sterling Publishing Company, Inc.
387 Park Avenue South, New York, N.Y. 10016
© 1994 by John A. Nelson
Distributed in Canada by Sterling Publishing
% Canadian Manda Group, P.O. Box 920, Station U
Toronto, Ontario, Canada M8Z 5P9
Distributed in Great Britain and Europe by Cassell PLC
Villiers House, 41/47 Strand, London WC2N 5JE, England
Distributed in Australia by Capricorn Link (Australia) Pty Ltd.
P.O. Box 6651, Baulkham Hills, Business Centre, NSW 2153, Australia
Manufactured in the United States of America
All rights reserved

Sterling ISBN 0-8069-0644-8

Contents

INTRODUCTION

All the toys and puzzles in this book are designed to be made over a weekend—all fifty-two of them. A project for each weekend for a full year. I must admit, however, one or two of the projects may require a *long*, three-day weekend. Others can be put together in a weekend, but will need an extra day or two to apply a stain or paint finish. The projects range from very simple to an intermediate woodworking level—something for everyone, I hope!

The projects have been carefully chosen so that most can be made using only basic woodworking tools. A few projects do require a lathe, and one or two require the use of a band or scroll saw. If you do not have those power tools, but would like to make these projects, you might consider enrolling in an evening woodworking class for adults. Most local high schools offer these classes and have the special equipment you will need.

Because each reader will be at a different skill level and each will have completely different tools, only brief and basic instructions for making each project are given in most cases. Most projects are rather simple and, with a little thought and preparation, should be within the skill level of most woodworkers.

Each and every project has been made at least once using the finished plans and drawings, so all dimensions *should* be correct by now. We have checked and rechecked each dimension and all the detail illustrations, but Murphy's law will surely prevail, so *please* recheck each dimension again before you make any cuts yourself.

If the toys are for very young children take extra care not to have any small pieces that could break off. You can also use the toilet-roll-tube test—if a piece fits through a cardboard toilet-roll tube, then it is too small and not safe.

Using the Drawings for Each Project

With each project there is at least a two-view drawing provided. One is almost always called the *front view*, and the other is either the *side view* or the *top view*. These views are positioned in a standard way; the front view is always the most important view and the place you should start in studying the drawings. The side view is located directly to the *right* of the front view; the top view is located directly *above* the front view.

At times a *section view* is used to further illustrate some particular feature(s) of the project. The section view is sometimes a partial view that illustrates only a portion of the project such as a particular moulding detail or way of joining parts.

Most of the projects also have an *exploded view*, which fully illustrates how the project goes together. Make sure that you understand how the project is to be assembled *before* any work is started.

The drawings throughout this book *number* each and every part. Each part is called off in as many views as possible so that you can see *exactly* where each part is located. A box accompanies each set of drawings that serves as a *bill of materials* list. Each part is listed, *in order*, using the same number *and* noting its name, its overall size, and exactly *how many* of each part is required.

Multiple parts should be made exactly the same size and shape. Every now and then a project requires a *pair* of parts, that is, a right-hand piece and a left-hand piece. In such a case, take care not to make duplicate pieces, but rather a left-hand and right-hand pair. In most projects requiring a pair, this is noted—but for any "multiple" parts double-check if in doubt.

Throughout, when practical, I numbered all the parts in the order that I would *suggest* you make and assemble them. You might want to make and assemble your project some other way, but this is what worked best for me and is how I made it.

Making the Project

After you thoroughly study the project, start by carefully making each individual part. Take care to make each piece exactly to the correct size and exactly *square*—that is, each cut at 90 degrees to the face—as required.

Sand each individual piece, but take care to keep all the edges sharp—*do not round the edges* at this time—some will be rounded *after* assembly.

After all the pieces have been made with great care, "dry-fit" the pieces—that is, cautiously put together the entire project to check for correct fit throughout before final assembly. If anything needs refitting, this is the time to correct it.

When the pieces all fit correctly, glue and/or nail the project together, again taking care that all fits are tight and square. Sand the project all over; it is at this time that edges can be "rounded," if necessary. The project is then ready for finishing.

Today, the trend is towards using the metric system of measure; therefore, a Metric Conversion chart is provided for quick conversion.

Enlarging a Pattern or Design

Many of the drawings are reduced relative to the actual size of the parts so that all of the information can be presented on the page. In some projects, the patterns for irregular parts or irregular portions of parts must be enlarged to full size. A grid of squares is drawn over these parts and the original size of the grid is noted on the drawing.

There are four commonly used ways a design or shape of the irregular part or parts can be enlarged to full size.

Method One

One of the simplest and most inexpensive ways is to use an ordinary office-type photocopy machine. Most of these newer machines have an enlarging/

reducing feature. Simply put the book page on the machine, choose the enlargement mode you need (usually expressed as a percentage of the original), and make a copy. In extreme cases, you may have to make *another* enlarged copy of the enlargement in order to get the required size—sometimes you must make more than two copies. In some cases you will not be able to get the exact required size but the result will be close enough for most work, perhaps requiring a little touching up, at most.

Method Two

A very quick and extremely accurate method is to go to a local commercial "Quick Printer" and ask them to make a P.M.T. (photomechanical transfer) of the area needed to be enlarged or reduced. This is a photographic method that yields an *exact* size without any difficulty. This method is much more expensive than making a photocopy. But, depending on the size of the final P.M.T., if your time is valuable, it might be worth the cost. The Photograph Puzzle, Project 29, must be enlarged using this method.

Method Three

Another simple, quick method is to use a drawing tool called a *pantograph*. It is an inexpensive tool that is very simple to use for enlarging or reducing to almost any required size. If you do a lot of enlarging or reducing, the cost of this tool may be worth the price.

Method Four

Most authors assume woodworkers will use the grid and dot-to-dot method. It is very simple; you do not have to be an artist to use the method. This method can be used to enlarge or reduce to *any* size or scale. This method requires eight simple steps:

♦**Step 1** Note what size the full-size grid should be—this is usually indicated on the drawing near the grid. Most of the grids used with the project drawings must be redrawn so that each square is one-half inch or one inch per side.

♦**Step 2** Calculate the overall required width and height. If it is *not* given, simply count the squares across and down and multiply by the size of each square. For example, a one-half inch grid with 15 squares across requires an overall width of 7½ inches. The paper size needed to draw the pattern full size should be a little larger than the overall size of the part.

♦**Step 3** Note: It would be helpful if you have a few basic drafting tools, but not necessary. Tools suggested are: a drafting board, a scale (ruler), a T-square, a 45-degree triangle, drafting tape, and a sheet of paper a little larger than the required overall size of the pattern. Tape the paper to the drafting board or other surface and carefully draw the required grid on the paper using the drafting tools or whatever tools you have.

♦**Step 4** On the original reduced drawing in the book, start from the upper left corner and add *letters* across the top of the grid from left to right, A through whatever letter it takes to get to the other side of the grid. From the same starting point, add *numbers* down, from 1 to whatever number it takes to get to the bottom of the grid.

♦**Step 5** On your full-size grid, add letters and numbers in exactly the same way as the original.

♦**Step 6** On the original reduced drawing, draw dots along the pattern outline wherever it crosses the grid.

♦**Step 7** On your full-size grid, locate and draw the same dots on the grid. It is helpful to locate each dot by using the letters across the top and the numbers along the side. For example, a dot at B-6 can easily be found on the new, full-size grid by coming down from line B and over on line 6.

♦**Step 8** All that is left to do is to connect the dots. Note: you do not have to be exact, all you have to do is to sketch a line between the dots using your eye to approximate the shape of the original reduced drawing.

Transferring the Pattern from Paper to Wood

Tape the full-size pattern to the wood with carbon paper in between for transferring the pattern. If you are going to copy the pattern many times, make a template instead. Simply transfer the pattern onto a sheet of heavy cardboard or ⅛-inch-thick hardboard or plywood, and cut out the pattern. This template can then be used over and over by simply tracing around the template to lay out the pattern for each copy.

If the pattern is symmetrical—that is, the exact same size and shape on both sides of an imaginary line—make only a *half-pattern* and trace it twice, once on each side of the midline. This will ensure the perfect symmetry of the finished part.

For small patterns—8½ inches by 11 inches or smaller at full size—make a photocopy of the pattern. Using rubber cement or spray-mount adhesive, lightly glue the copy directly to the wood. Cut out the piece with the copy glued directly to the wood. Simply peel the copy from the wood *after* you cut out the piece. Then sand all over.

Selecting Material for Your Project

As lumber will probably be the most expensive material you will purchase for each project, it is a good idea that you have some basic knowledge about lumber so that you can make wise choices and save a little money here and there on your purchases.

All lumber is divided into two kinds, hardwood and softwood. Hardwoods are deciduous trees, trees that flower and lose their leaves seasonally; softwoods are the coniferous trees, which are cone-bearing and mostly evergreen. In actuality, a few "hardwoods" are softer than some "softwoods"— but on the whole, hardwoods are harder, closer grained, much more durable, tougher to work, and take a stain beautifully. Hardwood typically costs more than softwood, but it is well worth it.

All wood contains pores—open spaces that served as water-conducting vessels—which are more noticeable in some kinds than in others. Woods such as oak and mahogany have pores that are very noticeable and probably should be filled, for the best finished appearance. Woods such as maple and birch have what is called close-grain, which provides a beautiful smooth finish.

The *grain* of wood is the result of each year's growth of new cells. Around the tree's circumference each year annular growth forms a new and hard fibrous layer. Growth in most trees is seasonal but somewhat regular, so that these rings are evenly spaced. In other trees this annular growth is not very regular, thus creating uneven spacing and thickness. The patterns formed by the rings when the tree is cut into lumber is what we see as the grain pattern.

The softwoods I used for some of the projects are pine, spruce, and fir. Pine was the favorite since it is the easiest to work. The hardwoods I used most were maple, walnut, oak, cherry, poplar, and birch. As most projects will not use much material and will probably be subjected to hard use, I highly recommend using hardwood whenever possible.

Always buy "dried" lumber, since "green" lumber will shrink, twist, and warp while drying. Purchase the best lumber you can find for these projects since each of them does not take much material at all. Your work will be much easier and the finished project will be so much better for the better-quality wood. The actual cost difference between an inexpensive piece of wood and the best you can find will be quite small since the overall cost of any of these projects is very low to begin with. Some projects use plywood—if you use plywood, use a high-grade, multi-ply plywood.

Gluing

Wood glues are either "hot" or "cold" glue, depending whether or not heat is used to prepare them. The "hot" glue is made from animal parts, which make the glue very strong and quick-setting. Until very recently old-fashioned hide glue was considered the *only* true, satisfactory kind of glue to use in cabinetmaking. Recent developments in new and better "cold" glues have made this generalization debatable. Cold glues are all derived from synthetic material of one kind or another. They vary in durability and strength. For the simpler projects cold glue is, by far, the easiest to use, and I recommend its use. In using cold glue, always follow the instructions given on the label.

When gluing, always take care to clean all excess glue from around the joint. This is a *must* if you are going to stain the project. The excess glue will not take the stain and will appear white. I find that by waiting for 10 to 15 minutes, just until the glue is almost set, I can carefully remove most of it with a sharp wood chisel. Do not wipe off the excess glue with a wet cloth since the water will weaken the glue joint and possibly spread glue into the pore space irretrievably, staining the wood.

For the few projects that are a little difficult to hold together properly while gluing, a hot-glue gun can be very helpful. Hot-glue guns use solid glue sticks that are inserted, heated to their melting point, and then liquid glue is pushed through the tip while very hot. This kind of glue dries very quickly and sets in about 10 seconds without clamping. Take care if you use this kind of glue since it is difficult to get good, tight-fitting joints every time. The glue sets up so quickly that you have to work very fast. This kind of glue is good to use for special applications but not for everything; the slower-drying cold glue is still better to use for most of the projects.

Finishing

Once you have completed assembling your project, you are then ready to apply a finish. This is the important part and should not be rushed. Remember, this is the part that will make the biggest impression for many years to come. No matter how good the wood and hardware you use, regardless of how good the joints are, a poor finish will ruin your project. If it takes eight hours to make the project, plan on eight hours to finish it correctly.

Preparing

◆**Step 1**   All joints should be checked for tight fits. If necessary apply water putty to all joints—allow ample time for drying. Set and fill the nail heads with water putty.

◆**Step 2**   Sand the project all over in the direction of the wood grain. If sanding is done by hand, use a sanding block, and be careful to keep all corners still *sharp*. Sand all over using an 80-grit sandpaper. Resand all over using a 120-grit sandpaper, and, if necessary, sand once more with 180-grit sandpaper. Take care not to "round" edges at this time.

◆**Step 3**   If you do want any of the edges rounded, use the 120-grit sandpaper, and later the 180-grit sandpaper, specifically to round the edges.

Staining Your Toys and Puzzles

There are two major kinds of stain: water-base stain and oil-base stain. Water stains are commonly purchased in powder form and mixed as needed by dissolving the powder in hot water. Premixed water-base stains are now also widely available. Water stain has a tendency to raise the grain of the wood, so that after it dries, the surface should be lightly sanded with fine sandpaper. Oil stain is made from pigments ground in linseed oil and does not raise the grain.

◆**Step 1**   Test the stain color on a scrap piece of the same kind of lumber to make certain it will be the color you wish.

◆**Step 2**   Wipe or brush on the stain as quickly and as evenly as possible to avoid overlapping streaks. If a darker finish is desired, apply more than one coat of stain. Try not to apply too much stain on the end grain. Allow to dry in a dust-free area for at least 24 hours.

Transparent Finishes for Your Toys and Puzzles

Shellac is a hard, easy-to-apply finish and dries in a few hours. For best results, thin slightly with alcohol and apply an extra coat or two. Several coats of thin shellac are much better than one or two thick coats. Sand lightly with extra-fine sandpaper between coats, but be sure to rub the entire surface with a dampened cloth. Strive for a smooth, satin finish or a high-gloss finish coat, as desired.

Varnish is easy to brush on and dries to a smooth, hard finish within 24 hours. It makes an excellent finish that is transparent and will give a deep finish look to your project. Be sure to apply varnish in a completely dust-free area. Apply one or two coats directly from the can with long, even strokes. Rub between each coat, and after the last coat, with 0000 steel wool.

Oil finishes are especially easy to use for projects such as those in this book. Oil finish is easy to apply, long-lasting, never needs resanding, and actually improves wood permanently. Apply a heavy, wet coat uniformly to all surfaces, and let set for 20 or 30 minutes. Wipe completely dry until you have a pleasing finish.

Painting Your Toys and Puzzles

Use a high-quality paint, either oil or water base. Today, the trend is towards water-base paint. Prime your project, and lightly sand after it dries. Apply two *light* coats of paint rather than one thick coat. I like to add some water to thin water-base paint since I feel that water-base paint tends to be a little thick. As these projects are for children, be sure to use a *nontoxic* paint at all times. There are a lot of special high-gloss paints available—consider using them on some of your projects.

◆**Note** For a very satisfying "feel" to the finish and a professional touch to your project, apply a top coat of paste wax as the final step.

THE 52 TOY & PUZZLE PROJECTS

TOYS OF TODAY

1 ◆ Toy Soldier

All toy project books must have a toy soldier—here's my version. This toy soldier requires a lathe to produce, and is a "fun" turning project.

Instructions

◆1 Cut the pieces to overall size. Be sure to add a little extra length to each piece to hold them between lathe centers.

◆2 Turn all pieces, approximately as shown.

◆3 Sand each piece before removing it from the lathe, as you would for any project.

◆4 Drill the ⅛-inch, ¼-inch, and two ⅝-inch-diameter holes in the body, part number 1.

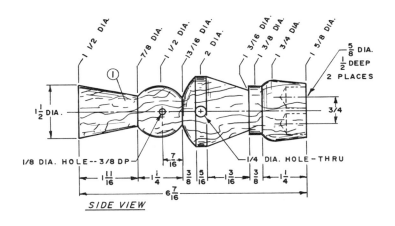

SIDE VIEW

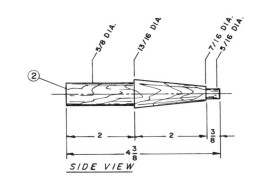

SIDE VIEW

NO.	NAME	SIZE	REQ'D.
1	BODY	2 DIA. X 6 7/16 LG.	1
2	LEG	13/16 DIA. X 4 3/8 LG.	2
3	ARM	3/4 DIA. X 3 1/4 LG.	2
4	FOOT	7/16 X 5/8 - 1 9/16	2
5	TOP - CAP	3/8 DIA. X 1 3/8 LG.	1
6	NOSE	1/8 DIA. - 5/8 LG.	1
7	ARM AXLE	1/4 DIA. - 3 5/8 LG.	1

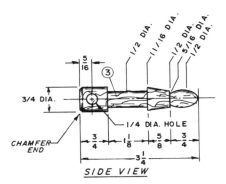

SIDE VIEW

♦5 Drill the ¼-inch-diameter hole in the arms, parts number 3.

♦6 Cut the two feet to size, and drill a 5/16-inch-diameter hole in each, as shown.

♦7 Assemble all pieces. Glue the arms, parts number 3, to the arm axle, part number 7, but *not* to the body. (This allows the arms to move.)

♦8 Prime all over for painting. (Continued on next page.)

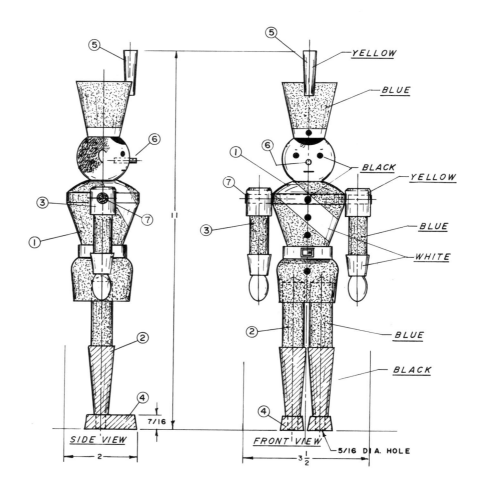

♦9 Paint according to the suggested colors or to suit. Be sure to use a nontoxic paint.

♦10 Apply a top coat of clear, water-base varnish, if you wish.

2♦Merry-Go-Round on String

This is a copy of an old toy design. There are many versions, and almost any animal could be substituted, if you wish. To make the merry-go-round work, simply wind it up (backwards) and release. You can leave your animals with a natural wood color or paint them as you desire.

Instructions

♦1   Cut all pieces to overall size.

♦2   Using a compass, lay out the base, top support, and ground pieces, parts number 1, 2, and 3. (Set your compass at 2½ inches, 1¾ inches, and 2¾ inches to get the 5-inch, 3½-inch, and 5½-inch diameters.)

♦3   Locate and drill the required holes in parts number 1, 2, and 3.

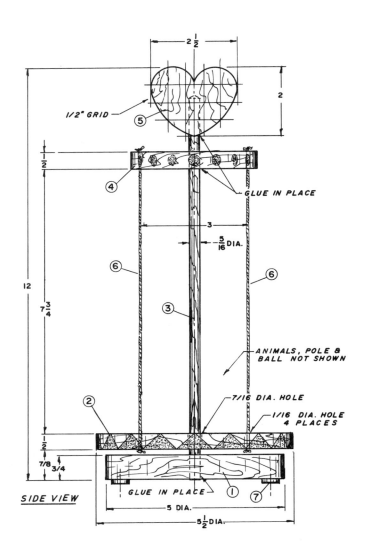

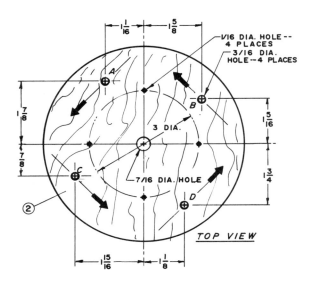

NO.	NAME	SIZE	REQ'D.
1	BASE	3/4 X 5 SQUARE	1
2	GROUND	1/2 X 5 1/2 SQUARE	1
3	CENTER POLE	5/16 DIA.– 11 LONG	1
4	TOP SUPPORT	1/2 X 3 1/2 SQUARE	1
5	HEART	1/2 X 2 1/2–2 LG.	1
6	TWINE	11 LONG	4
7	FOOT FELT	1/2 DIA.	4
8	CAMEL	1/2 X 2 1/2–3 LG.	1
9	GRAFFEE	1/2 X 2 1/4 – 4 3/16	1
10	HIPPO	1/2 X 2 – 4 1/8 LG.	1
11	ELEPHANT	1/2 X 3 1/8–4 LG.	1
12	POST	3/16 DIA. X 4 LONG	4
13	SPHERE	1/2 DIA.	4

♦4   On a ½-inch grid, lay out the animals and heart, parts number 8, 9, 10, 11, and 5.

♦5   Cut out the animals and heart. Drill the vertical holes for the posts, parts number 12, and the pole, part number 3.

♦6   Drill the ³/₁₆-inch-diameter holes in the top balls, parts number 13.

♦7   Dry-fit all pieces. Disassemble.

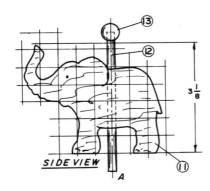

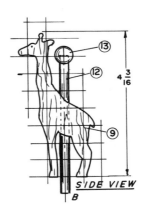

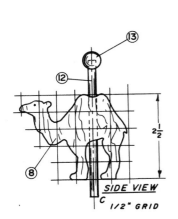

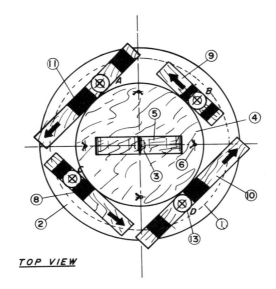

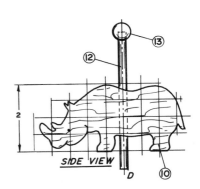

♦ 8   Prime and paint to suit. Be plain or fancy, whatever you prefer.

♦ 9   Glue pieces together *after* painting.

♦ 10   Cut 4 pieces of twine, parts number 6, approximately 11 inches long.
Add the string, and check that the assembly turns freely.

3♦Crayon Tractor-Trailer

This toy truck is great for your budding *artist*. It provides a handy place to hold crayons, when they're not in use. It can be made out of a piece of 2-inch by 4-inch wood.

Instructions

♦1   Cut pieces to overall size.

♦2   Carefully lay out the cab, part number 1, and box, part number 2.

♦3   Drill all required holes, as shown.

♦4   The wheels, parts number 4, can be cut from a 1½-inch-diameter dowel (½ inch wide) or you can purchase 1½-inch-diameter wheels.

♦5   Dry-fit all pieces.

♦6   You can leave the truck natural or paint it as you wish.

♦7   Paint to suit, and assemble.

♦8   Glue the wheels to the axles. Let them turn freely inside the cab or box.

♦9   Add a set of crayons, and the tractor-trailer is ready for that artist.

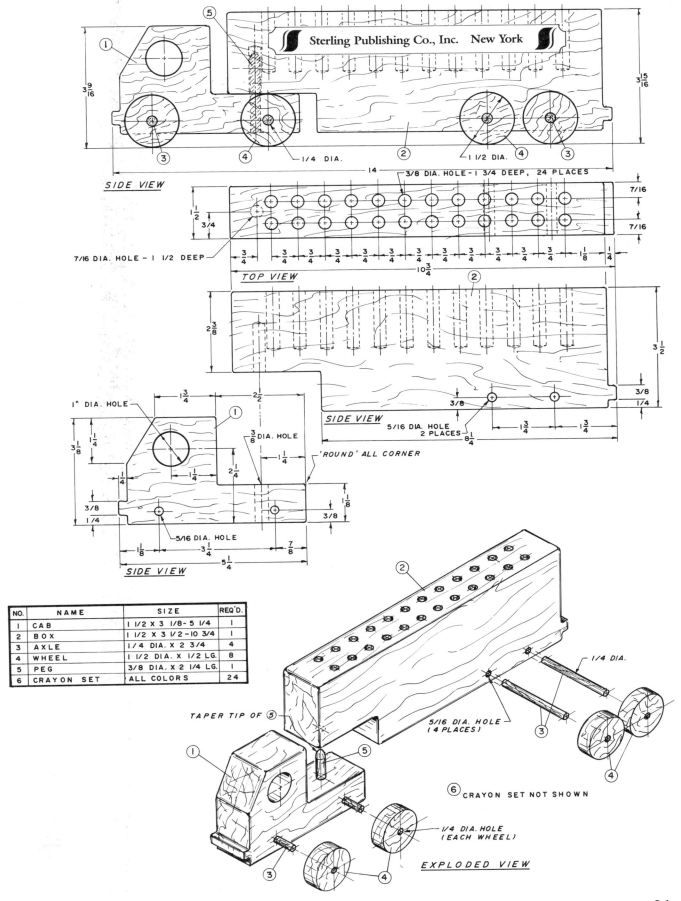

NO.	NAME	SIZE	REQ'D.
1	CAB	1 1/2 X 3 1/8 - 5 1/4	1
2	BOX	1 1/2 X 3 1/2 - 10 3/4	1
3	AXLE	1/4 DIA. X 2 3/4	4
4	WHEEL	1 1/2 DIA. X 1/2 LG.	8
5	PEG	3/8 DIA. X 2 1/4 LG.	1
6	CRAYON SET	ALL COLORS	24

Sterling Publishing Co., Inc.   New York

SIDE VIEW

TOP VIEW

SIDE VIEW

SIDE VIEW

EXPLODED VIEW

4◆Train with Passengers

One of the most popular toys ever is the toy train. All toy projects books must have a train set. I tried to come up with a simple train that could be made up of all those scrap pieces of wood you usually burn up or throw away. I chose modern, round magnets and tacks to hook the train cars together. This project can be left natural or painted.

Instructions

◆1   Cut all pieces to overall size. (See numbered parts cutting list.)

◆2   Glue up required pieces as necessary.

◆3   Drill all holes according to the sizes given.

◆4   Dry-fit all pieces.

◆5   Glue up each car (refer to the exploded view). Don't forget to add the passengers.

◆6   The wheels can be cut from a 1-inch-diameter dowel (³⁄₁₆ inch thick) or you can purchase 1-inch wheels. (Add wheels to cars last.)

◆7   Paint cars to suit or leave them natural. Add the magnets. Don't forget to use the magnets "north" to "south" so that the cars will attach correctly.

◆8   Paint and add wheels; check that they turn freely.

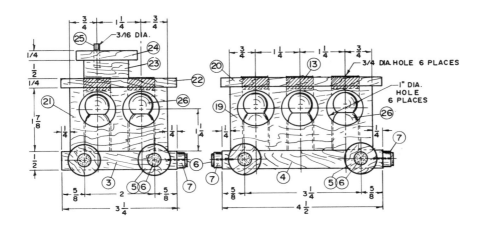

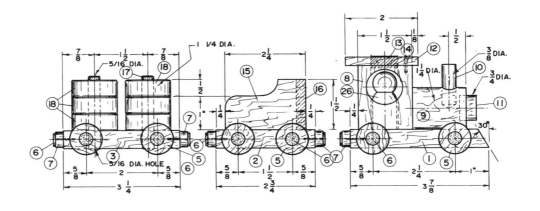

NO.	NAME	SIZE	REQ'D.
1	BASE	1/2 X 1 3/4 – 3 7/8 LG.	1
2	BASE	1/2 X 1 3/4 – 2 3/4 LG.	1
3	BASE	1/2 X 1 3/4 – 3 1/4 LG.	2
4	BASE	1/2 X 1 3/4 – 4 1/2 LG.	1
5	WHEEL	1" DIA. X 3/16 LG.	20
6	TACK	–	28
7	MAGNET	1/2 DIA	8
8	CAB	3/4 X 1 1/2 – 1 7/8	2
9	BOILER	1 1/4 DIA. – 1 1/2 LG.	1
10	CHIMNEY	3/8 DIA. – 1 1/8 LG.	1
11	LIGHT	3/4 DIA. – 1/2 LG.	1
12	ROOF	1/4 X 1 3/4 – 2 LG.	1
13	PLUG	3/4 DIA. – 7/16 LG.	6
14	GUIDE	CUT FROM 6d NAIL	1
15	SIDE	1/4 X 1 1/2 – 2 1/4	2
16	FRONT	1/4 X 1 1/2 – 1 LG.	1
17	SUPPORT	5/16 DIA. – 2 1/8	2
18	CARGO	1 1/4 DIA. – 1/2 LG.	6
19	CAB	3/4 X 1 7/8 – 4 LG.	2
20	ROOF	1/4 X 1 3/4 – 4 1/2	1
21	CAB	3/4 X 1 7/8 – 2 3/4	2
22	ROOF	1/4 X 1 3/4 – 3 1/4	1
23	LOOKOUT	1/2 X 3/4 – 1 1/4 LG.	1
24	ROOF	1/4 X 1 – 1 3/4 LG.	1
25	CHIMNEY	3/16 DIA. – 3/4 LG.	1
26	PASSENGER	11/16 DIA. – 1 3/4	6

(Exploded view is on next page.)

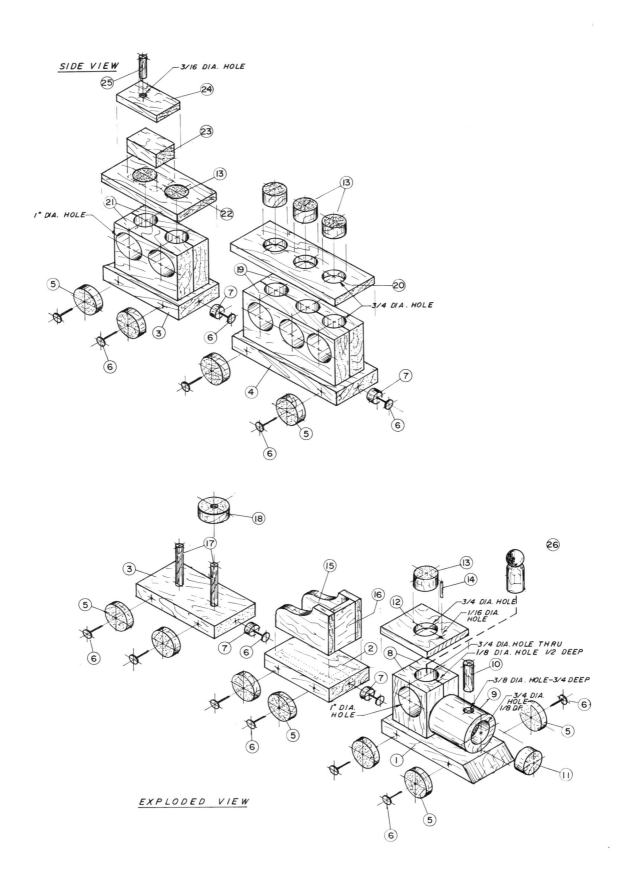

SIDE VIEW

3/16 DIA. HOLE

25

24

23

13

13

21

1" DIA. HOLE

22

13

19

20

3/4 DIA. HOLE

5

3

6

7

6

4

7

6

5

6

18

17

3

15

16

13

26

14

5

12

3/4 DIA. HOLE

1/16 DIA. HOLE

6

7

6

8

3/4 DIA. HOLE THRU
1/8 DIA. HOLE 1/2 DEEP

7

2

10

3/8 DIA. HOLE-3/4 DEEP

6

1" DIA. HOLE

9

3/4 DIA. HOLE 1/8 DP.

6

5

1

11

6

5

EXPLODED VIEW

24

5 ♦ Tool Box with Tools

Here is a great project for your child or grandchild that is both fun and educational. This is a good project for girls as well as boys. When my three daughters were little they would work along with me helping to make various woodworking projects. They still recall how much they enjoyed making them.

I suggest you make the tool box first, then the tools.

Instructions

♦ 1   Cut all pieces to size according to the cutting list.

♦ 2   Lay out the ends, parts number 1, and cut them out making two pieces exactly the same.

♦ 3   Locate and drill a ¾-inch hole for the handle.

♦ 4   Nail all pieces together with the finishing nails, parts number 5. Check that everything is square.

♦ 5   Sand all over, rounding the edges slightly.

♦ 6   The hammer can be made out of simple dowels and shaped, as shown.

♦ 7   The screwdriver can also be made out of dowels and shaped as shown.

♦ 8   The saw and the square should be laid out and made according to the given dimensions. (Continued on the following two pages.)

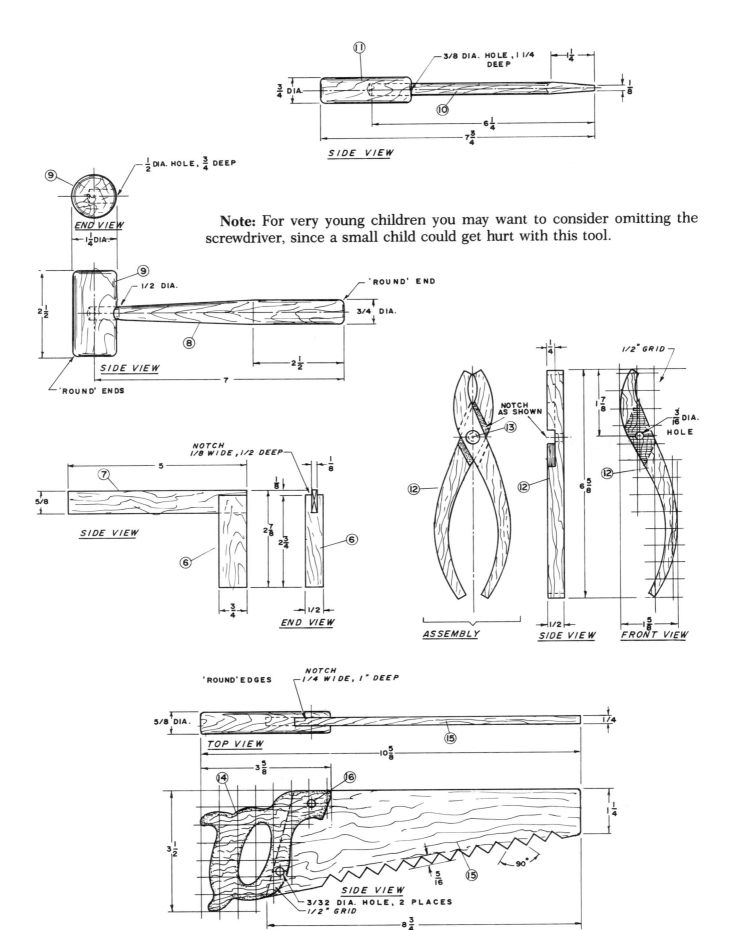

Note: For very young children you may want to consider omitting the screwdriver, since a small child could get hurt with this tool.

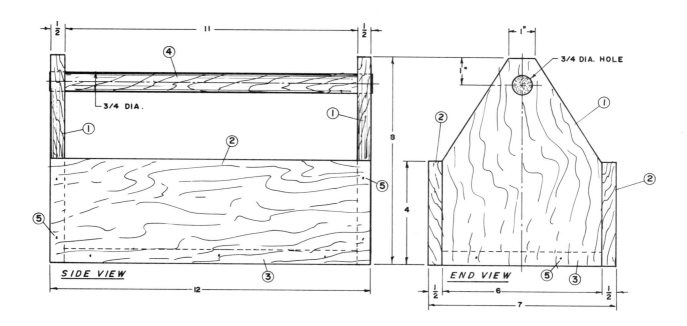

NO.	NAME	SIZE	REQ'D.
1	END	1/2 X 6 - 8 LONG	2
2	SIDE	1/2 X 4 - 12 LONG	2
3	BOTTOM	1/2 X 6 - 11 LONG	1
4	HANDLE	3/4 DIA. X 12 LG.	1
5	NAIL - FINISH	6 d	18
6	HANDLE	1/2 X 3/4 - 2 3/4	1
7	BLADE	1/8 X 5/8 - 5 LG.	1
8	HANDLE	3/4 DIA. - 7 LONG	1
9	HEAD	1 1/4 DIA. - 2 1/2 LG.	1
10	BLADE	3/8 DIA. - 6 1/4 LG.	1
11	HANDLE	3/4 DIA. - 2 1/2 LG.	1
12	HANDLE	1/2 X 1 5/8 - 6 5/8	2
13	PIN	3/16 DIA.	1
14	HANDLE	5/8 X 3 1/2 - 3 5/8	1
15	BLADE	1/4 X 3 1/8 - 8 3/4	1
16	PIN	3/16 DIA. X 5/8 LG.	2

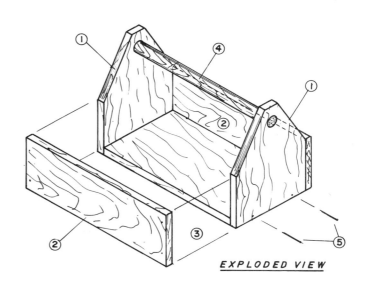

EXPLODED VIEW

♦9   The only tricky tool to make is the pliers.

♦10   On a half-inch grid lay out the jaws and cut, as shown. The left and right jaws are the same.

♦11   Locate and drill the 3/16-inch-diameter hole.

♦12   Locate and notch as shown—check again that you have a left and right jaw, each the same as the other.

♦13   Add the pin. (An axle pin used in holding wheels on toys makes a great pin for the pliers.) In gluing the pin in place, apply glue to the back jaw only so that the jaws operate freely.

♦14   Sand all over, rounding all corners.

♦15   Either paint or leave natural. I recommend that you paint the tool box with bright colors. The handle of screwdriver and the square can be painted yellow. Everything else will look great left natural with a clear top coat.

6 ♦ Log Cabin

As a child one of my favorite toys was a set of logs that kept me busy for hours. Naturally, this is one of my favorite projects. I also think this is one of the most educational toys in this book, since it teaches children to think and use their imagination. Many different structures can be built using these logs in various combinations. A special dado head and router bit will be needed for this project.

Important: In cutting the dadoes extreme care must be taken especially for the smaller parts. Use clamps, stops, or whatever else you have in cutting all dadoes. Be sure, as always, to wear safety glasses when making this project.

Instructions

♦ 1   Cut overall sizes exactly to ¾ inch by ¾ inch and 5-foot or 6-foot lengths. Be sure to use knot-free, straight-grained wood. Cut about twice as much material as you think you will actually need.

♦ 2   Set up the router to make the curved cuts, and run all the stock through at the same time at the same setting. (See "Figure A.")

Note: Multiple parts must be exactly the same size and shape; therefore, use whatever stops or jigs you have at your disposal.

♦ 3   Square one end.

♦ 4   Locate and cut ¾-inch-wide dadoes exactly ³⁄₁₆ inch deep, as shown.

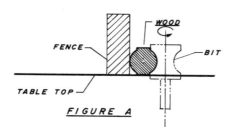

FENCE

WOOD

BIT

TABLE TOP

FIGURE A

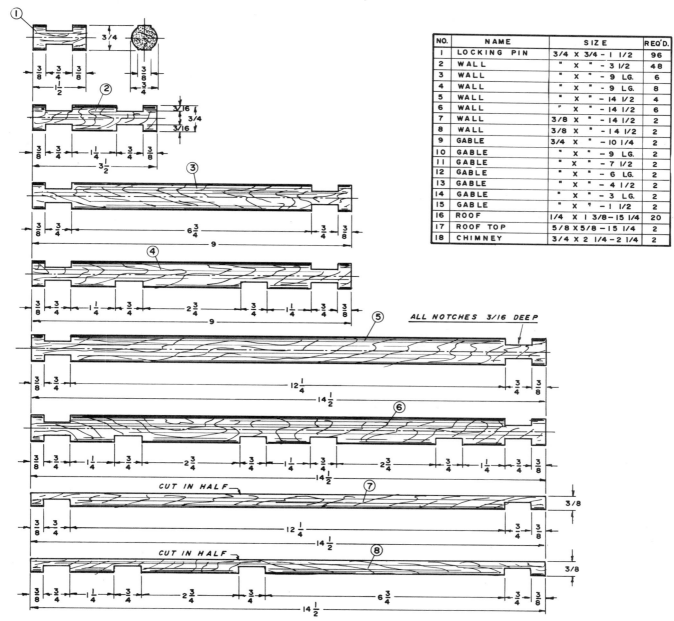

ALL NOTCHES 3/16 DEEP

CUT IN HALF

CUT IN HALF

NO.	NAME	SIZE	REQ'D.
1	LOCKING PIN	3/4 X 3/4 - 1 1/2	96
2	WALL	" X " - 3 1/2	48
3	WALL	" X " - 9 LG.	6
4	WALL	" X " - 9 LG.	8
5	WALL	" X " - 14 1/2	4
6	WALL	" X " - 14 1/2	6
7	WALL	3/8 X " - 14 1/2	2
8	WALL	3/8 X " - 14 1/2	2
9	GABLE	3/4 X " - 10 1/4	2
10	GABLE	" X " - 9 LG.	2
11	GABLE	" X " - 7 1/2	2
12	GABLE	" X " - 6 LG.	2
13	GABLE	" X " - 4 1/2	2
14	GABLE	" X " - 3 LG.	2
15	GABLE	" X " - 1 1/2	2
16	ROOF	1/4 X 1 3/8 - 15 1/4	20
17	ROOF TOP	5/8 X 5/8 - 15 1/4	2
18	CHIMNEY	3/4 X 2 1/4 - 2 1/4	2

♦5 Cut to specified length, again using stops to ensure uniformity.

Note: All dadoes are made before each piece is cut to final length in order to give you something to hold on to while making the dado cuts. *Again*, take extreme care; these cuts could be dangerous.

♦6 Sand all over, removing any sharp edges. (Continued on next page.)

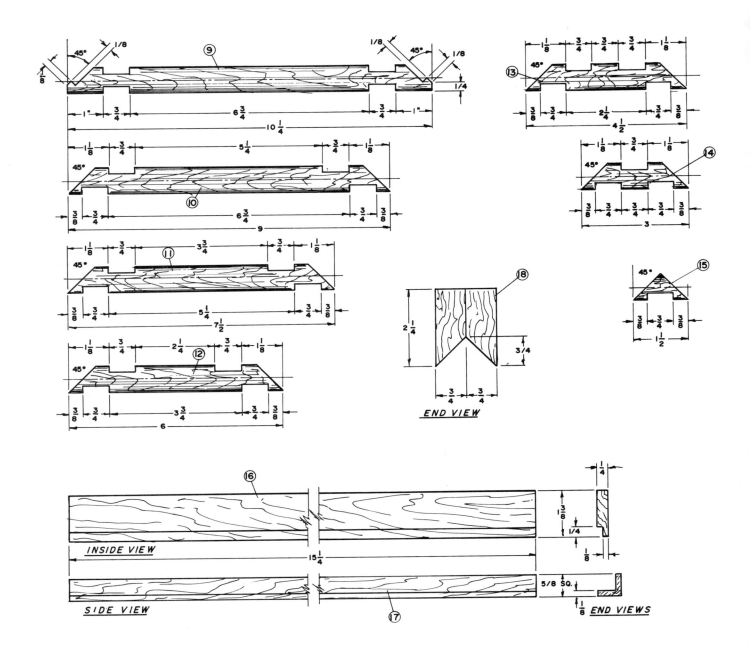

♦7 Roofing material, parts number 16 and 17, and chimney, part number 18, should be made as shown.

♦8 I recommend that you stain all the logs with a light walnut stain. Because there are so many pieces you might want to consider just dipping them in a can of stain.

♦9 Paint roof material green or any color of your choice.

♦10 Paint the chimney red.

7♦Pushcart

Here's a toy cart that can be used for almost anything from dolls to blocks or toy soldiers. Simple construction is used throughout, for easy assembly. It even has a built-in stand. (Mom might want to use it as a planter.)

Instructions

♦1   Cut all parts to overall size.

♦2   Assemble the body using parts number 1, 2, 3, and 4.

♦3   Add the support and axle support, parts number 5 and 6.

♦4   Add the pull, part number 7. I suggest that you glue and nail the pull in place.

♦5   Cut the wheels exactly to a 3-inch diameter, and drill a hole in the center of each for the screws.
(Continued on the following two pages.)

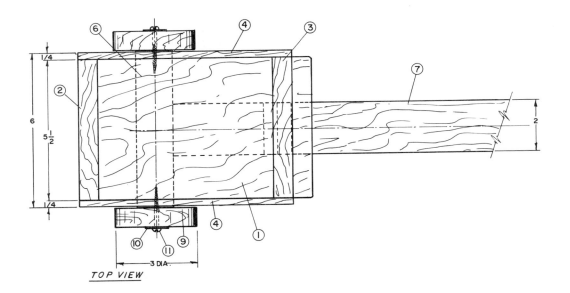

TOP VIEW

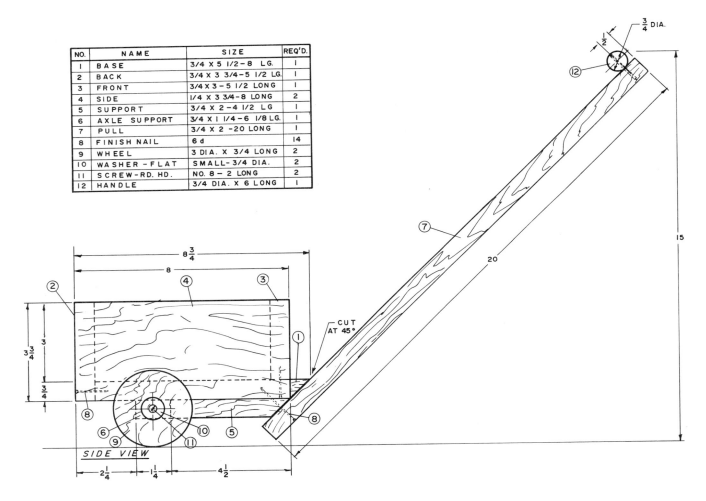

NO.	NAME	SIZE	REQ'D.
1	BASE	3/4 X 5 1/2 - 8 LG.	1
2	BACK	3/4 X 3 3/4 - 5 1/2 LG.	1
3	FRONT	3/4 X 3 - 5 1/2 LONG	1
4	SIDE	1/4 X 3 3/4 - 8 LONG	2
5	SUPPORT	3/4 X 2 - 4 1/2 LG	1
6	AXLE SUPPORT	3/4 X 1 1/4 - 6 1/8 LG.	1
7	PULL	3/4 X 2 - 20 LONG	1
8	FINISH NAIL	6 d	14
9	WHEEL	3 DIA. X 3/4 LONG	2
10	WASHER - FLAT	SMALL - 3/4 DIA.	2
11	SCREW - RD. HD.	NO. 8 - 2 LONG	2
12	HANDLE	3/4 DIA. X 6 LONG	1

SIDE VIEW

CUT AT 45°

◆6 Temporarily add the wheels.

◆7 Glue and nail the handle, part number 12, in place.

◆8 Sand all over, removing all sharp edges.

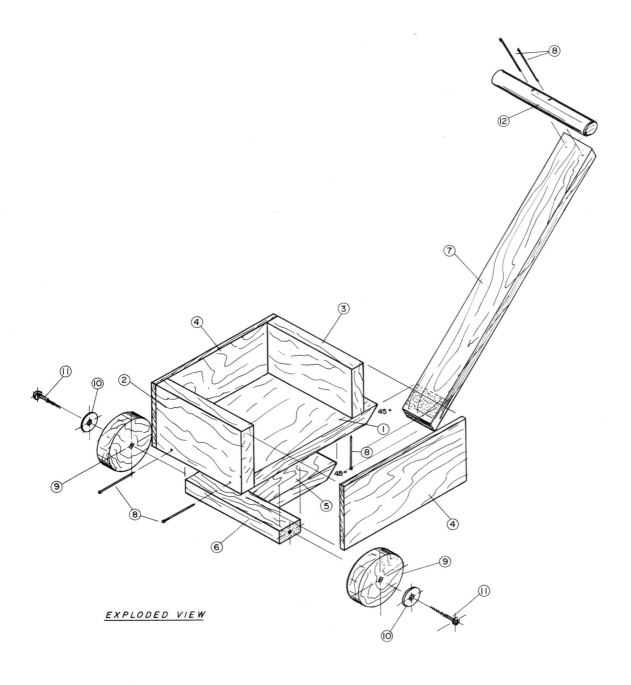

EXPLODED VIEW

♦ 9 Remove the wheels, and paint to suit using bright colors.

♦ 10 After the paint dries, attach the wheels, checking that they turn freely. The cart is ready for its cargo.

8 ♦ Circus Truck with Elephants

This exciting toy has a lot of possibilities. It includes circus elephants, and other animals from Project 41, Noah's Ark. This toy includes the bleachers, the circus ring, flags, sign, and spectators. You can embellish your circus in many ways, as large or as small as you wish. You can make it fancy with a lot of detail or keep it plain and simple. Whichever way you go, the circus is always exciting and lots of fun. If you listen carefully you can hear the circus band, smell the cotton candy, and see all the wild animals.

Note: The circus truck is designed to carry the bleachers, circus ring, various flags, and a few spectators. Feel free to embellish your version by adding clowns, and whatever else you wish.

Instructions

♦1   Cut all the pieces to size according to the numbered cutting list.

Note: It is important that all major dimensions are followed so that everything fits together correctly.

♦2   Carefully lay out all holes and notches in the base, part number 1, using the given dimensions.

♦3   Carefully lay out and make parts for the cab, parts number 2, 3, 4, and 5. (Continued on the following three pages.)

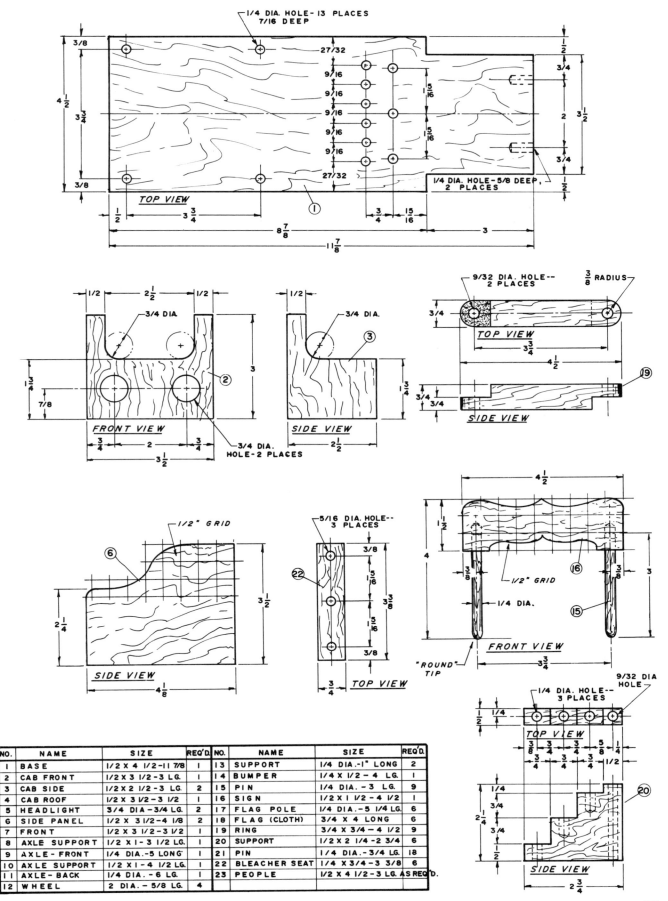

NO.	NAME	SIZE	REQ'D	NO.	NAME	SIZE	REQ'D
1	BASE	1/2 X 4 1/2-11 7/8	1	13	SUPPORT	1/4 DIA.-1" LONG	2
2	CAB FRONT	1/2 X 3 1/2-3 LG.	1	14	BUMPER	1/4 X 1/2 - 4 LG.	1
3	CAB SIDE	1/2 X 2 1/2-3 LG.	2	15	PIN	1/4 DIA. - 3 LG.	9
4	CAB ROOF	1/2 X 3 1/2-3 1/2	1	16	SIGN	1/2 X 1 1/2 - 4 1/2	1
5	HEADLIGHT	3/4 DIA-3/4 LG.	2	17	FLAG POLE	1/4 DIA.-5 1/4 LG.	6
6	SIDE PANEL	1/2 X 3 1/2-4 1/8	2	18	FLAG (CLOTH)	3/4 X 4 LONG	6
7	FRONT	1/2 X 3 1/2-3 1/2	1	19	RING	3/4 X 3/4 - 4 1/2	9
8	AXLE SUPPORT	1/2 X 1- 3 1/2 LG.	1	20	SUPPORT	1/2 X 2 1/4 -2 3/4	6
9	AXLE- FRONT	1/4 DIA.-5 LONG	1	21	PIN	1/4 DIA.- 3/4 LG.	18
10	AXLE SUPPORT	1/2 X 1- 4 1/2 LG.	1	22	BLEACHER SEAT	1/4 X 3/4 -3 3/8	6
11	AXLE- BACK	1/4 DIA. - 6 LG.	1	23	PEOPLE	1/2 X 4 1/2-3 LG.	AS REQ'D.
12	WHEEL	2 DIA. - 5/8 LG.	4				

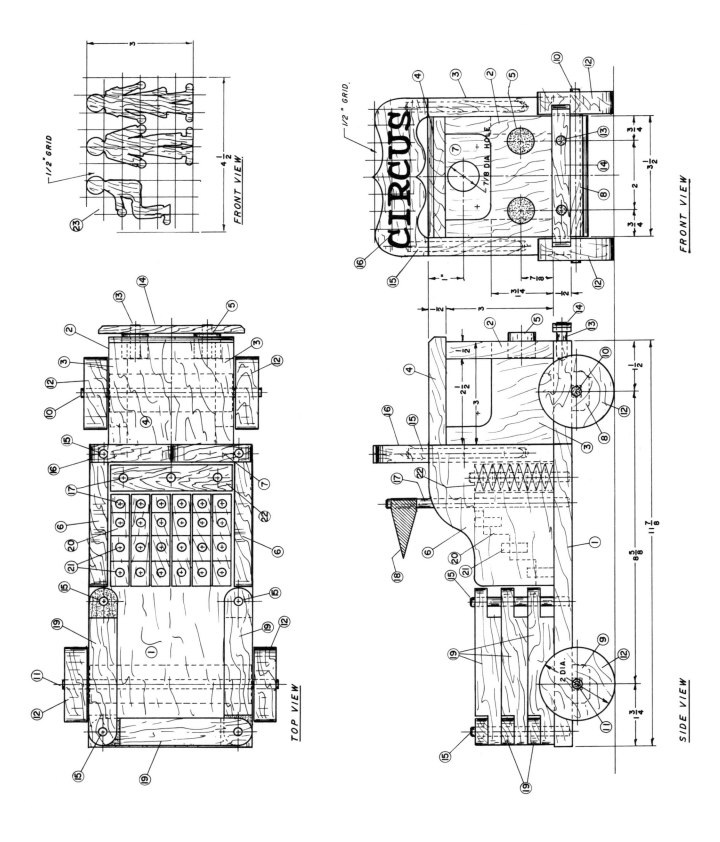

♦4 Lay out and cut parts for the truck bed, parts number 6 and 7.

♦5 Cut the dado in the axle supports, parts 8 and 9. Glue these to the base, part number 1.

♦6 Glue the cab assembly and the bed assembly to base.

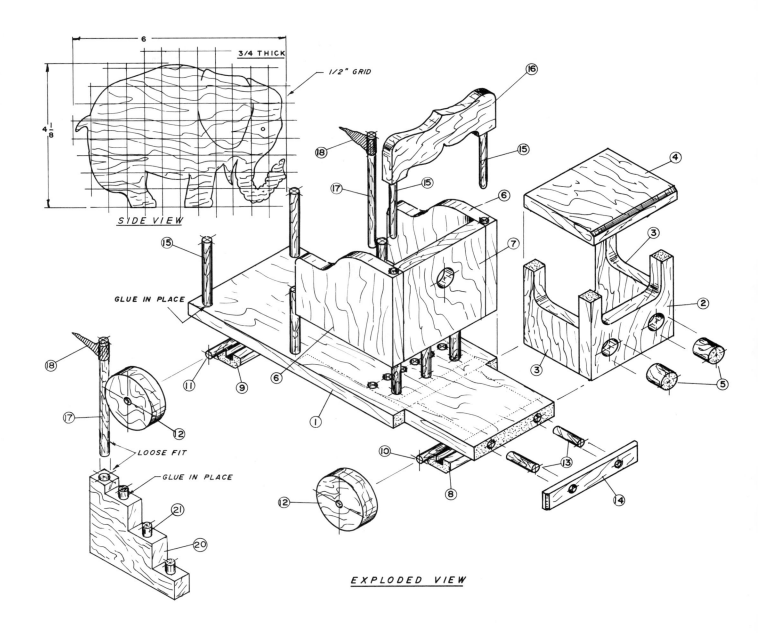

6
3/4 THICK
1/2" GRID
4 1/8
SIDE VIEW
GLUE IN PLACE
LOOSE FIT
GLUE IN PLACE
EXPLODED VIEW

♦ **7** Glue the various dowels in place, parts 13 and 15.

♦ **8** Add the bumper and the headlights, parts 5 and 14.

♦ **9** Temporarily add the wheels and axles, parts number 10, 11, and 12. (Glue the wheel axles only after painting.)

♦ **10** Cut to size and shape all the various miscellaneous pieces—for example, the grandstand, flagpoles, and people.

♦ **11** Paint all of the pieces with bright colors and with as much detail as you wish.

♦ **12** Cut out the elephant(s)—and as many animals as you wish from Project 41. Refer to the photograph for one possible setup of the grandstand and flags.

9♦Dog Bookrack, circa 1950

It could be said this project's "a dog"! Although not an actual toy, I feel children should be encouraged to read books as part of their play, so I am including this with the toys. If books are presented in a bright and cheery setting they may well be as appealing as a toy.

Instructions

♦1   Cut all pieces to overall size, according to the cutting list.

♦2   On a 1-inch grid lay out the detail of the various pieces.

♦3   Transfer the patterns to the wood, and carefully cut each piece out.

♦4   Sand all over.

♦5   Locate and drill all countersunk holes for the flathead screws, parts number 7.

♦6   The supports, parts number 6, are made from a thin piece of metal, approximately $\frac{1}{16}$ inch thick. If you don't have materials or tools to prepare these supports, any sheet-metal shop can cut them for you from pieces of scrap metal.

♦7   Assemble all pieces, keeping everything square.

♦8   Epoxy the metal supports to the bottom, as shown. (Continued on the next two pages with the exploded view on page 40.)

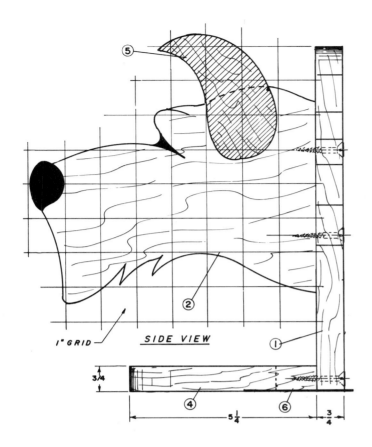

(5)

1" GRID

SIDE VIEW

(2)

1" GRID

3/4

(4)

(6)

(1)

5 1/4

3/4

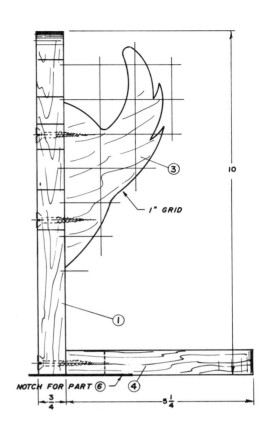

(3)

1" GRID

(1)

NOTCH FOR PART (6)

(4)

3/4

5 1/4

10

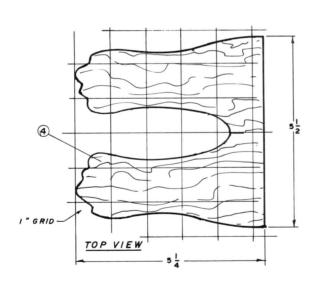

(4)

1" GRID

TOP VIEW

5 1/2

5 1/4

NO.	NAME	SIZE	REQ'D.
1	BODY	3/4 X 5 1/2 - 10 LG.	2
2	HEAD	3/4 X 6 - 8 LONG	1
3	TAIL	3/4 X 3 1/4 - 6 1/2	1
4	BASE (FOOT)	3/4 X 5 1/2 - 5 1/4	2
5	EAR	1/4 X 2 1/2 - 4 1/4	2
6	SUPPORT	1/16 X 5 1/2 - 6 LG.	2
7	SCREW - FL. HD.	NO. 8 X 2 LONG	8

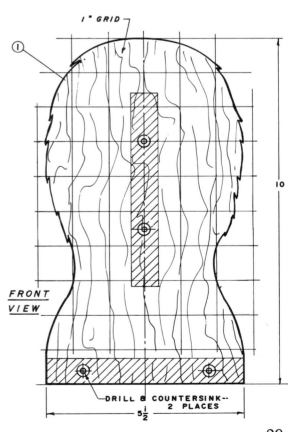

1" GRID

(1)

FRONT VIEW

10

DRILL & COUNTERSINK-- 2 PLACES

5 1/2

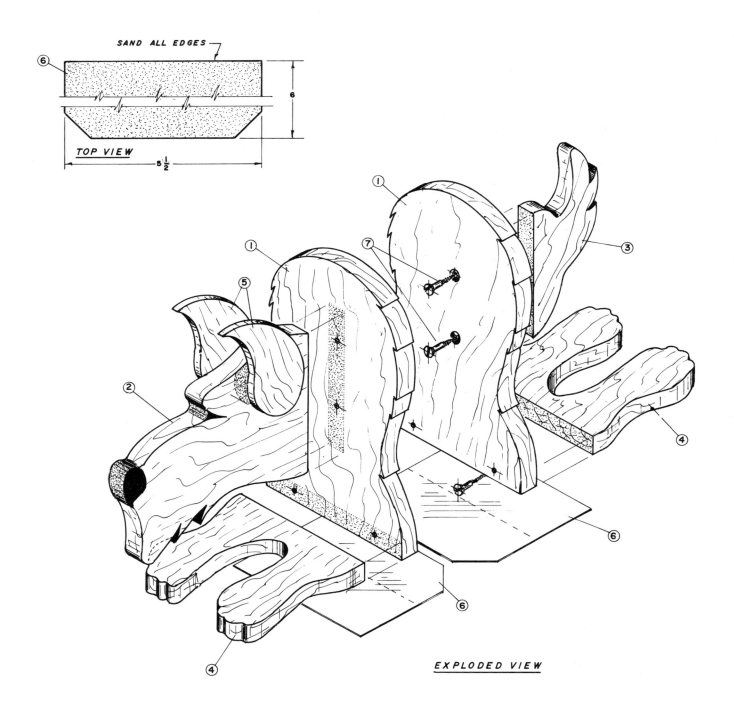

SAND ALL EDGES

TOP VIEW

EXPLODED VIEW

♦9 Resand all over and round slightly to remove all sharp edges.

♦10 Paint to suit.

10♦Doll Tricycle

Even dolls and teddy bears need a toy. So here is a toy for them. I suggest that you make this out of hardwood, especially the handlebars, part number 6.

Instructions

♦1   Cut all parts to overall size, according to the cutting list.

♦2   On a half-inch grid lay out the seat, and transfer the pattern to the wood.

♦3   Using a compass, lay out the axle support, part number 2, and handlebar, part number 6, according to the given dimensions.

♦4   Cut out the four 3-inch-diameter wheels, and drill holes in the center of each for the axles.

♦5   Complete all other pieces, according to the dimensions given.

♦6   Using a ⅛-inch cove cutter bit with a ball-bearing follower, rout the bottom of the seat and handlebars.
(Continued on the following two pages.)

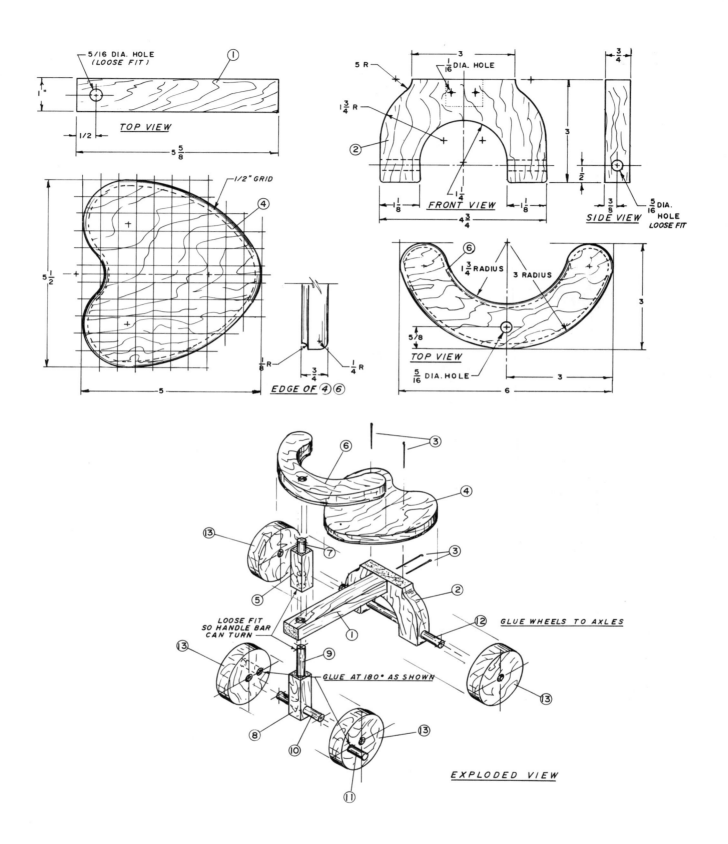

♦7 Using a ¼-inch-radius router bit, round the top edges of the seat and handlebars.

♦8 Assemble the tricycle using the exploded view. Check that the front wheels move and steer freely.

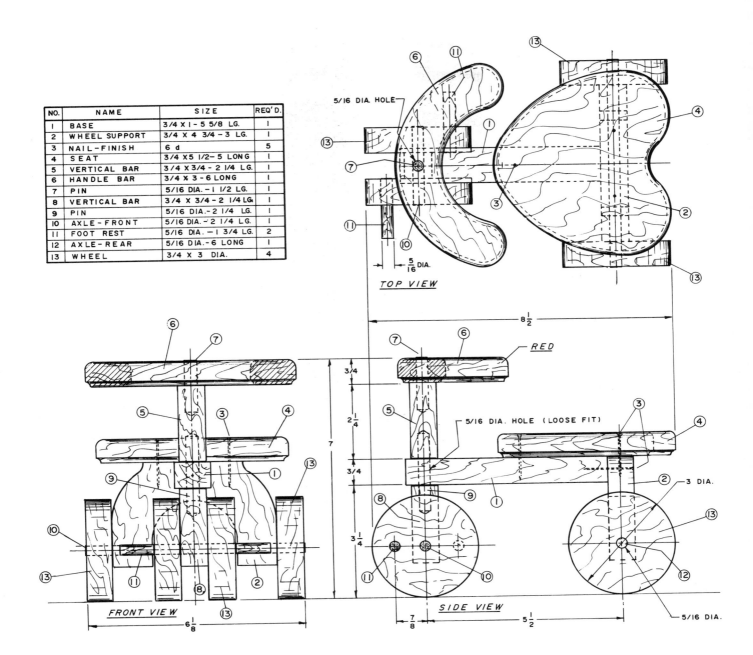

NO.	NAME	SIZE	REQ'D.
1	BASE	3/4 X 1 - 5 5/8 LG.	1
2	WHEEL SUPPORT	3/4 X 4 3/4 - 3 LG.	1
3	NAIL - FINISH	6 d	5
4	SEAT	3/4 X 5 1/2 - 5 LONG	1
5	VERTICAL BAR	3/4 X 3/4 - 2 1/4 LG.	1
6	HANDLE BAR	3/4 X 3 - 6 LONG	1
7	PIN	5/16 DIA. - 1 1/2 LG.	1
8	VERTICAL BAR	3/4 X 3/4 - 2 1/4 LG.	1
9	PIN	5/16 DIA. - 2 1/4 LG.	1
10	AXLE - FRONT	5/16 DIA. - 2 1/4 LG.	1
11	FOOT REST	5/16 DIA. - 1 3/4 LG.	2
12	AXLE - REAR	5/16 DIA. - 6 LONG	1
13	WHEEL	3/4 X 3 DIA.	4

◆9   Sand all over, removing all sharp edges.

◆10   Paint to suit, using bright colors.

11 ♦ Doll High Chair

This project makes a great toy for a doll or teddy bear—and, of course, a child.

Instructions

♦1   Cut all pieces to overall size, according to the cutting list.

♦2   Lay out the shape of the various pieces, using the given dimensions. The back, part number 9, will require being laid out on a 1-inch grid. The arm support and tray, parts number 14 and 15, will have to be laid out on a ½-inch grid.

♦3   Locate and drill all holes using the given directions.

♦4   Be sure to chamfer the four legs and two arms, as shown.

♦5   Glue the four pegs, parts number 3, to the seat, part number 1, as shown.

♦6   Dry-fit the legs and rails. Trim and fit to suit, keeping true to the overall dimensions.

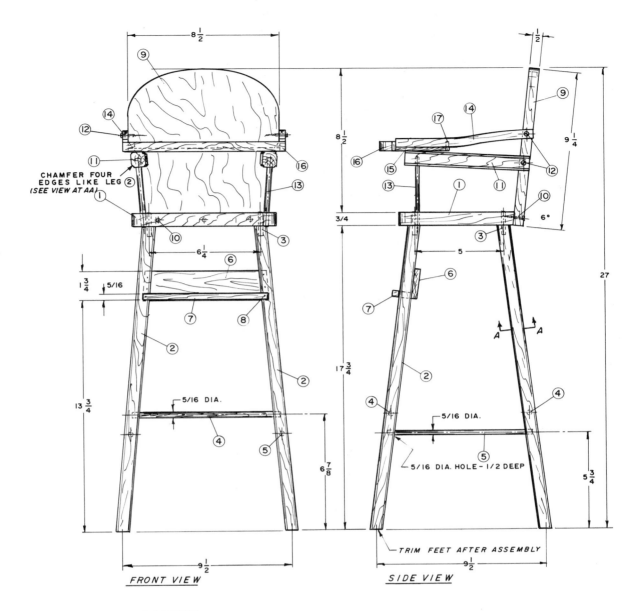

FRONT VIEW   SIDE VIEW

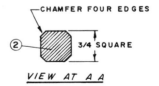

VIEW AT A A

CHAMFER FOUR EDGES

3/4 SQUARE

NO.	NAME	SIZE	REQ'D.
1	SEAT	3/4 X 6 3/8 – 8 1/8	1
2	LEG	3/4 X 3/4 – 18 LONG	4
3	PEG	1/4 DIA. – 1 1/2 LG.	4
4	RAIL (FRONT/BACK)	5/16 DIA. – 8 1/4 LG.	2
5	RAIL (SIDE)	5/16 DIA. – 8 1/8 LG	2
6	SUPPORT	1/4 X 1 3/4 – 7 5/8	1
7	FOOT REST	5/16 X 1 1/8 7 3/8	1
8	BRAD	3/4 LONG	5
9	BACK	1/2 X 8 1/2 – 9 3/8	1
10	SCREW – FL. HD.	NO. 6 – 1 1/4 LONG	3
11	ARM REST	7/8 X 7/8 – 7 1/8 LG.	2
12	SCREW – RD. HD.	NO. 6 – 2 LONG	4
13	POST	5/16 DIA. X 4 1/8 LG.	2
14	ARM SUPPORT	5/16 X 1 3/4 – 8 3/8	2
15	TRAY	1/8 X 3 1/2 – 8 1/2	1
16	FRONT RAIL	1/8 X 1/2 – 9 5/8 LG.	1
17	BACK RAIL	1/8 X 1/2 – 8 5/8 LG.	1

♦7 Trim off the bottom of the legs so that they are flush with floor.

♦8 Once everything fits properly, glue the assembly permanently together. (Continued on the following two pages.)

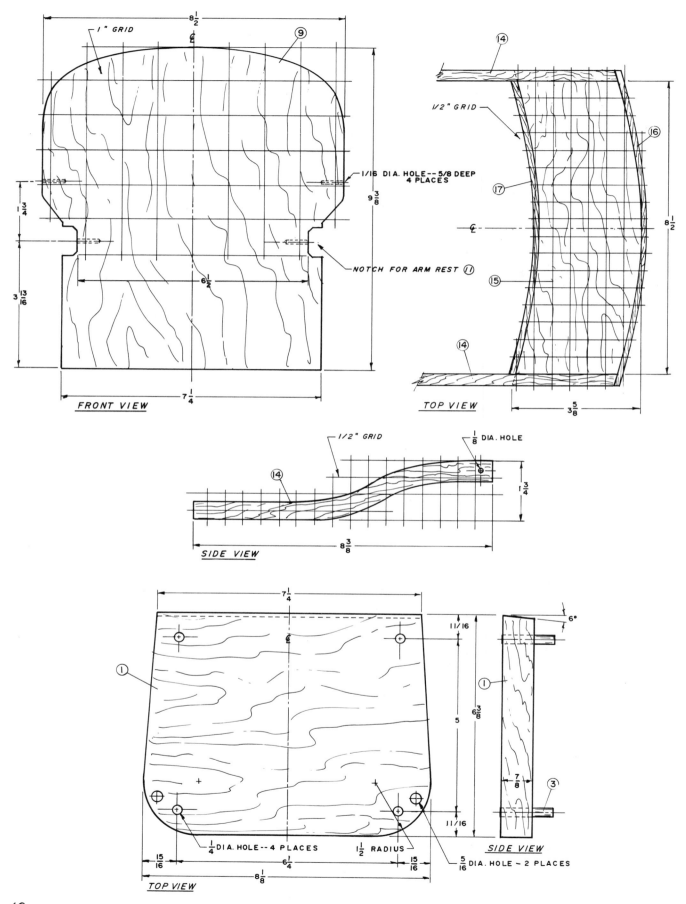

1" GRID

8 1/2

9

1/16 DIA. HOLE -- 5/8 DEEP
4 PLACES

9 3/8

1 3/4

3 13/16

6 1/2

NOTCH FOR ARM REST 11

7 1/4

FRONT VIEW

14

1/2" GRID

17

16

15

8 1/2

14

TOP VIEW

3 5/8

1/2" GRID

1/8 DIA. HOLE

14

1 3/4

8 3/8

SIDE VIEW

7 1/4

11/16

1

6 3/8

5

1

3

11/16

1/4 DIA. HOLE -- 4 PLACES

1 1/2 RADIUS

15/16

6 1/4

15/16

5/16 DIA. HOLE - 2 PLACES

8 1/8

TOP VIEW

6°

7/8

SIDE VIEW

46

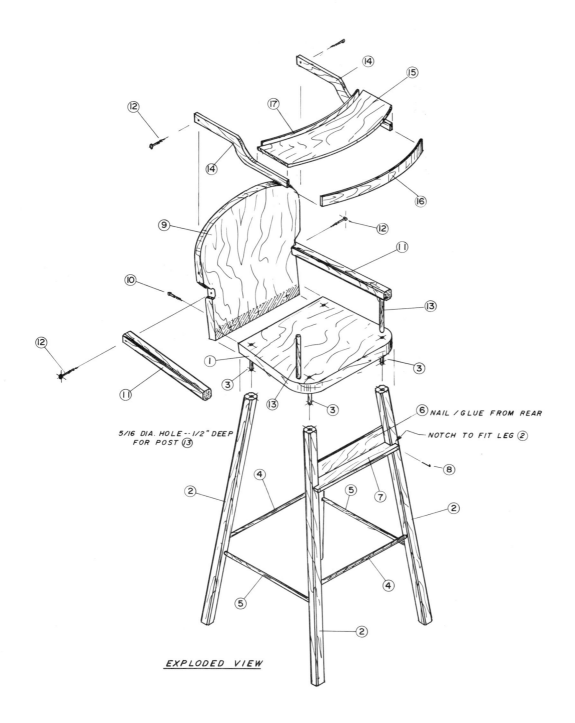

5/16 DIA. HOLE -- 1/2" DEEP
FOR POST ⑬

⑥ NAIL / GLUE FROM REAR

NOTCH TO FIT LEG ②

EXPLODED VIEW

♦9 Locate and assemble the support and the foot rest, parts number 6 and 7.

♦10 Put the tray assembly together as illustrated, and secure it to the chair with roundhead screws, parts number 12.

♦11 Lightly sand all over, removing sharp edges.

♦12 Prime and paint to suit. Take as many liberties as you wish in embellishing this project. You may want to pin-stripe it, put a tole-painted design on it, stencil it, etc.

When you are finished painting it the way you choose, it will be ready for your child's or grandchild's doll.

12 ♦ Child's Picnic Table

A few years ago I built a full-size picnic table for the patio. It came out great and we really enjoyed it. When the grandchildren came to visit it seemed a little overpowering for them. So I scaled the drawings down and came up with this model. Now when the grandchildren come to visit they have their own little table, and they just love it.

Instructions

♦1 Cut all parts to overall size, according to the cutting list.

♦2 Trim all parts using the end view of the table assembly as a guide.

♦3 Put together the two end assemblies using parts number 1, 2, 3, and 8. Be sure to keep the seat support and top support parallel.

♦4 Assemble the remaining parts of the table. Add the cross brace, part number 5, and the top brace, part number 4, as shown.

♦5 Cut a 1-inch by 1-inch chamfer at the outer edges of the top and seat, to eliminate any sharp edges. (Refer to the top view.)

♦6 Sand all over to remove any sharp edges.

♦7 Paint to suit.

Now your children or grandchildren have a table of their own to enjoy.

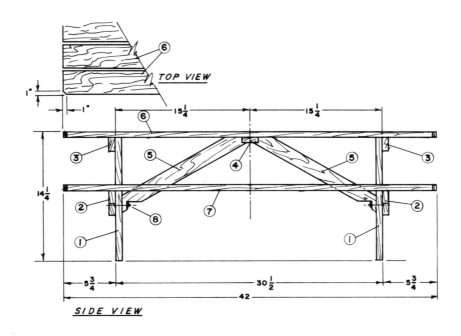

TOP VIEW

SIDE VIEW

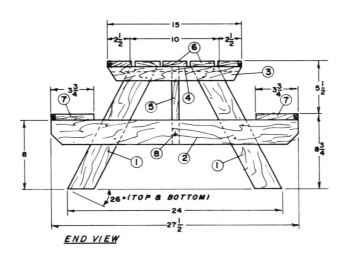

END VIEW

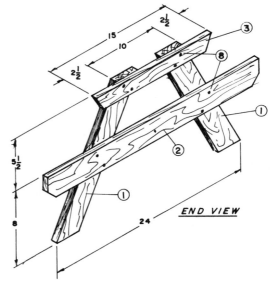

END VIEW

NO.	NAME	SIZE	REQ'D.
1	LEG	3/4 X 2 3/4 – 16 1/2	4
2	SEAT SUPPORT	3/4 X 2 3/4 – 27 1/2	2
3	TOP SUPPORT	3/4 X 1 3/4 – 15 LG.	2
4	BRACE	3/4 X 1 3/4 – 15 LG.	1
5	BRACE	3/4 X 1 3/4 – 16 LG.	2
6	TOP	3/4 X 2 1/2 – 42 LG.	5
7	SEAT	3/4 X 3 3/4 – 42 LG	2
8	STOVE BOLT / NUT	NO 10 X 2 LONG	18
9	NAIL – COMMON	4 d	30

PULL TOYS

13 ◆ Duck in Wagon

Here is a simple project that can be made from scrap pieces of wood and is a great toy for a toddler.

Instructions

◆1   Cut all parts to overall size, according to the cutting list.

◆2   Lay out and cut out the duck body and the wings, parts number 1 and 2.

◆3   Assemble the wagon using parts number 3, 4, and 5.

◆4   Locate and drill the two ⅛-inch-diameter holes for the axles.

◆5   The wheels are simple; cut from a ¾-inch dowel, ¼ inch thick.

◆6   Sand all over, removing any sharp edges.

◆7   Paint to suit.

◆8   Glue the wheels to the axles. Check to make sure that they turn freely.

◆9   Add twine, part number 8, and the pull, part number 9.

◆10   You may want to add a ribbon to the neck; this is optional.

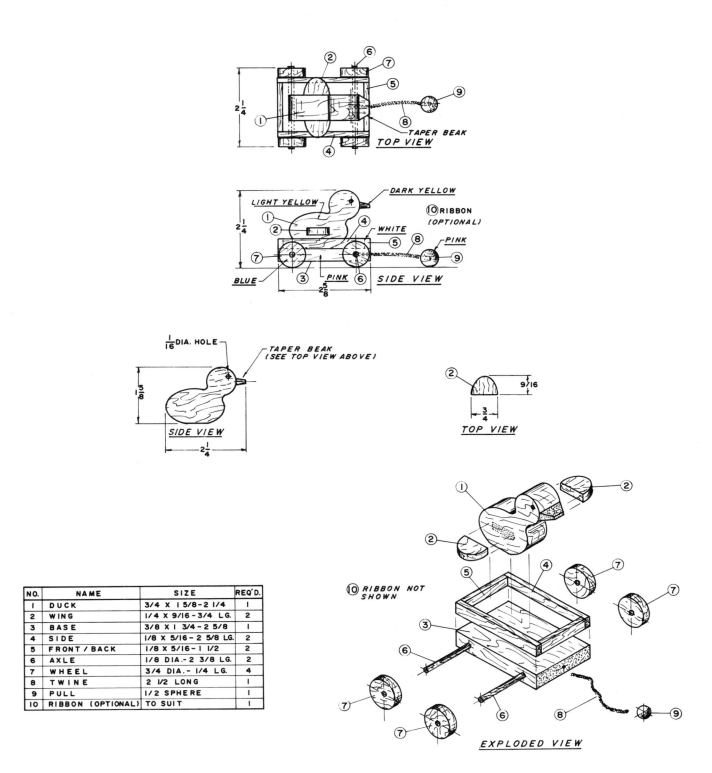

NO.	NAME	SIZE	REQ'D.
1	DUCK	3/4 X 1 5/8 - 2 1/4	1
2	WING	1/4 X 9/16 - 3/4 LG.	2
3	BASE	3/8 X 1 3/4 - 2 5/8	1
4	SIDE	1/8 X 5/16 - 2 5/8 LG.	2
5	FRONT / BACK	1/8 X 5/16 - 1 1/2	2
6	AXLE	1/8 DIA. - 2 3/8 LG.	2
7	WHEEL	3/4 DIA. - 1/4 LG.	4
8	TWINE	2 1/2 LONG	1
9	PULL	1/2 SPHERE	1
10	RIBBON (OPTIONAL)	TO SUIT	1

Important: If the pull toy is for a very young child, use a larger-diameter pull, part number 9, or a ³⁄₈-inch dowel approximately 3 inches long so there is no chance of the child swallowing it.

14 ◆ Rover, circa 1935

This is a copy of an original pull toy, circa 1935, that I found in an antique shop. It was a promotional toy for some company. The original one was painted lime green, thus the unusual lime-green color. You can paint yours any color you wish.

Instructions

◆1 Cut the parts to overall size.

◆2 The 2-inch-diameter wheels can be purchased or cut from a 2-inch dowel, 1 inch thick, as the original toy was. If made from a dowel use a ⅞-inch-diameter Forstner bit to counterbore ⅜ inch deep, as shown.

◆3 Using a 1-inch grid, lay out and cut out the body.

◆4 Locate and drill the ⅜-inch-diameter holes in the body and wheels.

◆5 Sand all over, removing any sharp edges.

◆6 Paint to suit.

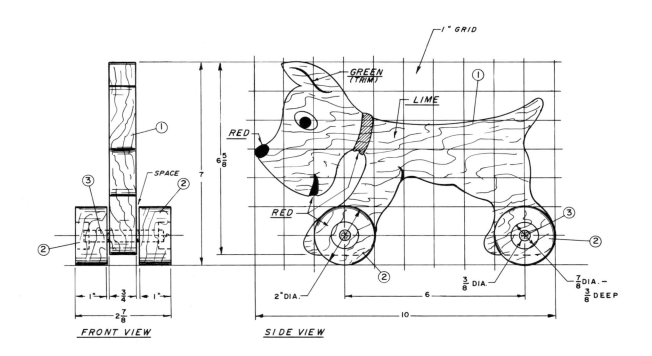

FRONT VIEW

SIDE VIEW

NO.	NAME	SIZE	REQ'D.
1	BODY	3/4 X 6 5/8 - 10 LG	1
2	WHEEL	2 DIA. X 1" THICK	4
3	AXLE	3/8 DIA. - 2 1/2 LG.	2

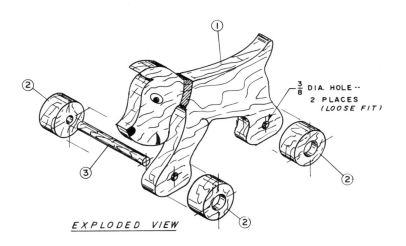

EXPLODED VIEW

15 ◆ Smiling Whale

There is something fishy about this project but it makes a great pull toy, anyway you look at it. Basically, it is made about the same way as the dog pull toy, Project 14. The basic difference is that there are spacers, parts number 3, used between the body and the wheels.

Instructions

◆1   Refer to Rover, Project 14, for instructions.

◆2   Paint your whale in whatever way you think it should be painted.

  Note: An optional hook, part number 5, can be made up instead of the simple pull string. This will make your "fish" a little more interesting— "the catch of the day."

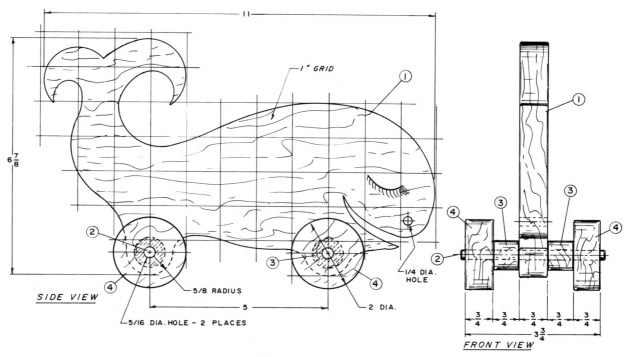

NO.	NAME	SIZE	REQ'D.
1	BODY	3/4 X 6 7/8 - 11 LG.	1
2	AXLE	5/16 DIA. - 4 LONG	2
3	SPACER	3/4 DIA - 3/4 LONG	4
4	WHEEL	2 DIA. - 3/4 LONG	4
5	FISH HOOK	3 1/4 LONG	1
6	HANDLE	5/8 DIA. - 3 1/2 LG	1
7	STRING	TO SUIT	1

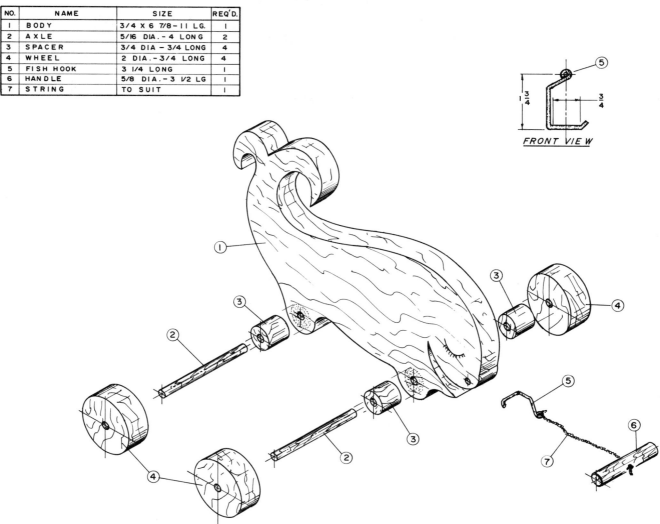

EXPLODED VIEW

16 ◆ Polly, the Pig

If you have always wanted a pet pig, here is your opportunity. Pigs make great pets. I know because I raised lots of them when I lived on a farm in northern Vermont. Contrary to popular belief, they are very clean animals and lots of fun.

This particular design is a take-off of an old folk-art pig design. I have noted the colors of the pig on the drawing; use them as you wish.

Instructions

◆**Note:** Since all pull toys are pretty much alike, refer to the general instructions for Rover, the pull toy, Project 14.

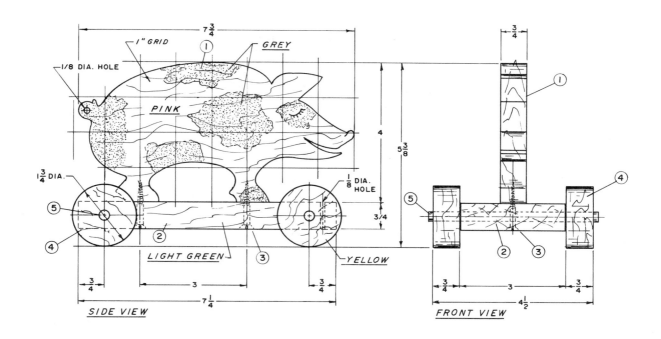

Side view and front view of toy pig on wheels with dimensions and color labels (GREY, PINK, LIGHT GREEN, YELLOW)

NO.	NAME	SIZE	REQ'D.
1	BODY	3/4 X 4 – 7 3/4 LG.	1
2	BASE	3/4 X 3 – 7 1/4 LG.	1
3	SCREW–FL. HD.	NO. 6–1 3/4 LONG	2
4	WHEEL	1 3/4 DIA.–3/4 LG.	4
5	AXLE	5/16 DIA.–4 5/8	2

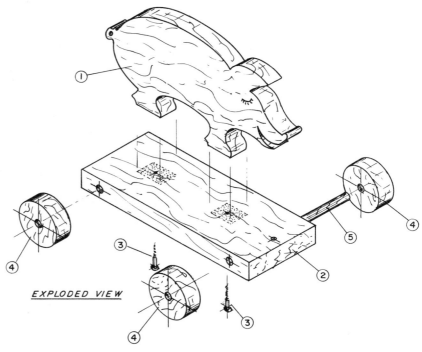

EXPLODED VIEW

17 ◆ Giraffe, circa 1920

I just took my granddaughter, Hilary, to the zoo this summer, and one of her favorite animals was the giraffe. She insisted I take a half-dozen photographs. After I got home and got thinking about it, I realized it would make a great toy for her and her brother to play with.

Instructions

Note: Follow the general instructions for Rover, Project 14, and refer to the exploded view.

If you want to make your giraffe match the look of the natural animal in the wild, find a picture of one in a book; copy and paint the details on your giraffe.

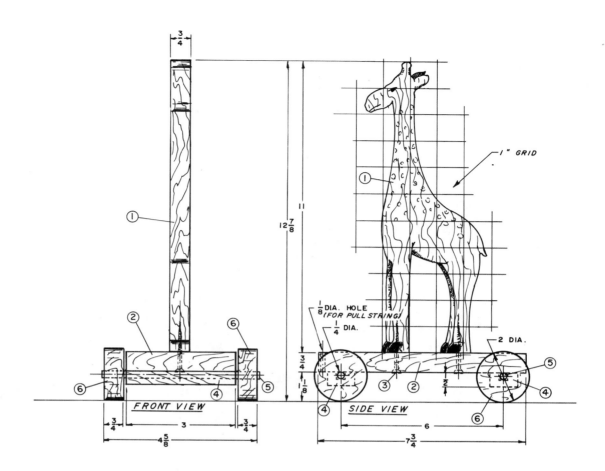

FRONT VIEW

SIDE VIEW

1" GRID

⅛ DIA. HOLE (FOR PULL STRING)

¼ DIA.

2 DIA.

NO.	NAME	SIZE	REQ'D.
1	BODY	3/4 X 5 3/4 – 11 LG.	1
2	BASE	3/4 X 3 – 7 3/4 LG.	1
3	SCREW — FL. HD.	NO. 8 – 2 1/2 LONG	2
4	AXLE SUPPORT	1/2 X 1 – 3 LONG	2
5	AXLE	1/4 DIA. X 4 3/4 LG.	2
6	WHEEL	2 DIA. X 3/4 THICK	4

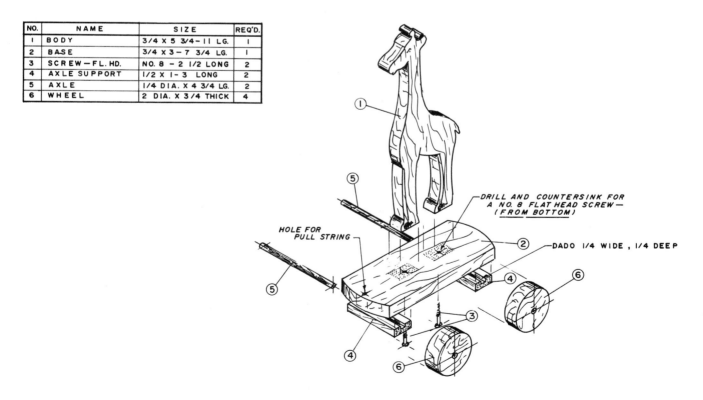

DRILL AND COUNTERSINK FOR A NO. 8 FLAT HEAD SCREW — (FROM BOTTOM)

DADO 1/4 WIDE, 1/4 DEEP

HOLE FOR PULL STRING

EXPLODED VIEW

18 ◆ Serpent

If you like creepy, crawly things, this one is for you. Use your imagination in making and painting this serpent, and you'll have a surefire winner.

Instructions

◆ 1   Using a ½-inch grid, lay out the body. Be sure to line up all the notches exactly as shown.

◆ 2   Before cutting the shape of the body out, carefully cut out all the notches.

◆ 3   Fit them all together. Tightly tape them together using masking tape.

◆ 4   With all three body pieces tightly taped together, locate the two ¼-inch-diameter holes for the two pins, parts number 4.

◆ 5   In the top surface, drill the two ¼-inch-diameter holes.

◆ 6   Take extra care to drill down as straight as possible.

◆ 7   Add the two ¼-inch-diameter pins, parts number 14.

◆ 8   Remove all masking tape, and transfer the body shape to the wood.

◆ 9   Carefully cut out the body pieces with the pins, parts number 4, still in place.

◆ 10   Sand all over. Taper the face and the end of the tail, as shown.

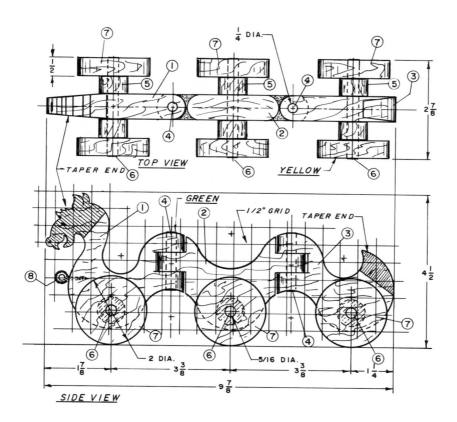

TOP VIEW

SIDE VIEW

NO.	NAME	SIZE	REQ'D.
1	HEAD	3/4 X 4 - 4 LONG	1
2	BODY	3/4 X 3 - 4 1/4 LG.	1
3	TAIL	3/4 X 3 - 3 1/2 LG.	1
4	PIN	1/4 DIA. X 1 3/4 LG.	2
5	SPACER	3/4 DIA. - 1/2 THICK	6
6	AXLE	5/16 DIA. X 3 LONG	3
7	WHEEL	2 DIA. X 1/2 THICK	6

♦11   Remove the pins and round the ends of the fingers and notches. Refer to the exploded view for details. Check that your joints move freely back and forth. File or sand, as necessary.

♦12   Locate and drill holes for the axles.

♦13   Two-inch-diameter wheels can be either made or purchased. (Continued on next page.)

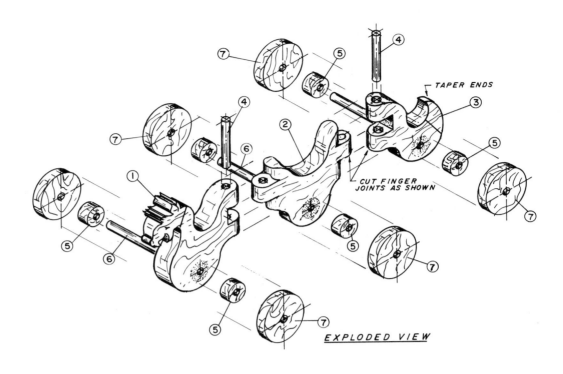

EXPLODED VIEW

♦14 Referring to the exploded view, assemble all parts.

♦15 Carefully glue the pins in place. Use glue sparingly so that you do not restrict joint movement.

♦16 Glue the wheels to the axles, again making sure you do not use too much glue. Make sure wheels turn freely.

♦17 Paint to suit, using the suggested colors, as you wish.
You now have your own Lake Champlain serpent.

19 ◆ Caterpillar

Children are fascinated with caterpillars; now they can have one of their own.

Instructions

◆1   Cut out all pieces to overall size. Sand all over.

◆2   Using the given dimensions, carefully lay out the body and head directly on the wood with a compass. Locate all holes, also.

◆3   Cut out the body and head.

◆4   Drill all 5/16-inch-diameter holes. I drilled these holes with a 3/8-inch diameter so that the axles would be "sloppy" in the holes and not bind.

◆5   Cut the spacers, parts number 4, from 1-inch-diameter dowel, 1/4 inch thick.

◆6   Since each wheel is a different diameter, each of the five pairs will have to be cut out individually.

◆7   Drill for the antennas, parts number 2.

◆8   Glue the spacers, parts number 4, onto the body, part number 1. You might have to redrill the 5 holes.

◆9   Drill a 1/8-inch-diameter hole for the nose.
(Continued on next page.)

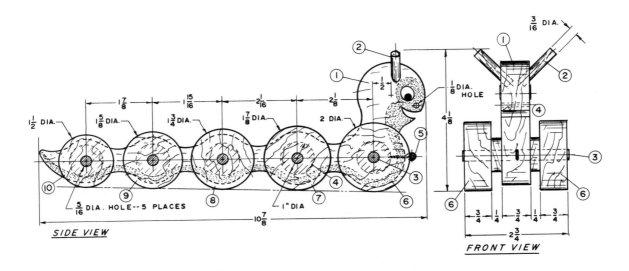

NO.	N A M E	S I Z E	REQ'D.
1	BODY	3/4 X 3 3/4 –10 7/8	1
2	ANTENNA	3/16 DIA– 1 1/4 LG.	2
3	AXLE	5/16 DIA.– 3 LONG	5
4	SPACER	1" DIA.– 1/4 LONG	10
5	EYE SCREW	SMALL	1
6	WHEEL 1	2 DIA. X 3/4 LG.	2
7	WHEEL 2	1 7/8 DIA. X 3/4 LG.	2
8	WHEEL 3	1 3/4 DIA. X 3/4 LG.	2
9	WHEEL 4	1 5/8 DIA. X 3/4 LG.	2
10	WHEEL 5	1 1/2 DIA. X 3/4 LG.	2

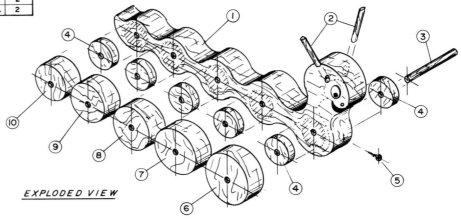

EXPLODED VIEW

♦ **10** Temporarily assemble all of the pieces. Check that everything fits correctly.

♦ **11** Disassemble and paint. Use your imagination; a caterpillar is typically green and yellow.

♦ **12** Assemble after painting and add the eye screw, part number 5, and string.

Just hope it doesn't turn into a butterfly!

20 ♦ Alligator, circa 1930

This is a copy of a circa 1930 folk-art toy I found in an antique shop. I thought it was great! It was definitely homemade, a bit crude, but a neat old toy. All joints are simple small eye screws with a wire for a pin. Refer to the exploded view. The jaw moves up and down as it rolls along. The jaw has an interesting hinge, part number 10, that I found especially unusual.

Instructions

♦1   Cut all pieces to overall size. (If you don't have a plane, substitute ¾-inch-thick wood in place of the ⅝-inch-thick.)

♦2   On a ½-inch grid, lay out the body pieces, parts number 1, 2, 3, 4, and 9. Note the ⅝-inch-wide by ⁵⁄₁₆-inch-deep notches in parts number 1, 4, and 9.

♦3   Transfer the patterns to the wood and cut out. (The front axle support has an extra notch.)

♦4   Sand all over. "Round" all edges slightly.

♦5   Glue the axle supports to the body. Check that they are square (90 degrees).

♦6   Add all eye screws as shown, except the four holding the front axle in place.

♦7   Assemble the jaw, part number 2, to the head, part number 1, with a wire, part number 10. Bend over after assembly.

♦8   Form the front axle, part number 7, as shown. (A coat hanger wire works great for this.)

♦9   Locate and drill four small holes in the front axle support for the four eye screws, parts number 5.

♦10   Assemble the drive rod, part number 8, to the front axle and *hammer* the four eye screws into the front axle (into the four small holes drilled in Step 9). (Continued on the two following pages.)

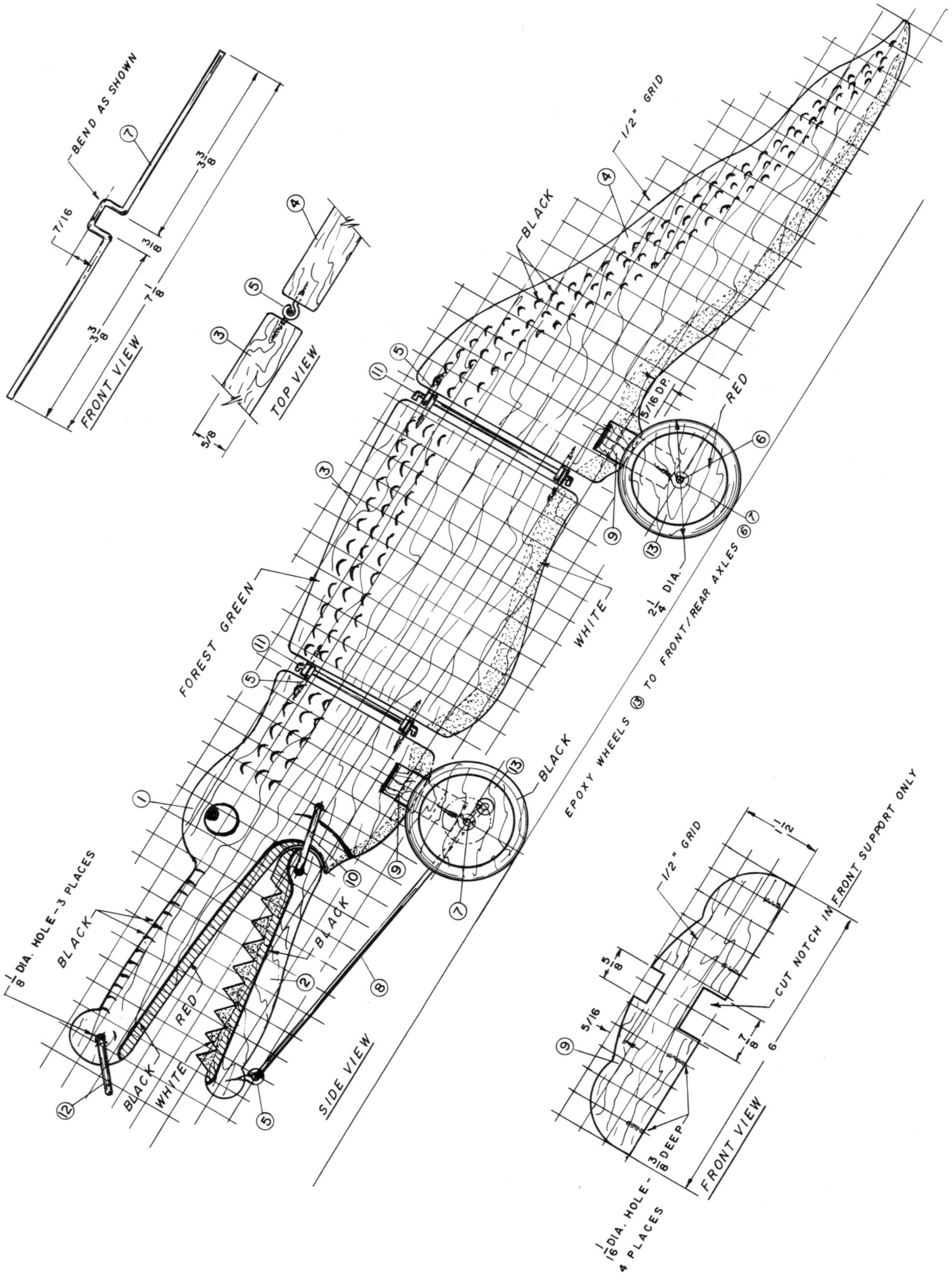
BEND AS SHOWN
7/16
$3\frac{3}{8}$
$\frac{3}{8}$
$3\frac{3}{8}$
$7\frac{1}{8}$
FRONT VIEW
TOP VIEW
$\frac{5}{8}$
1/2" GRID
BLACK
FOREST GREEN
WHITE
RED
5/16 DP.
$2\frac{1}{4}$ DIA.
EPOXY WHEELS ⑬ TO FRONT/REAR AXLES ⑥⑦
BLACK
$\frac{1}{8}$ DIA. HOLE - 3 PLACES
BLACK
BLACK
RED
BLACK
WHITE
SIDE VIEW
1/2" GRID
$1\frac{1}{2}$
CUT NOTCH IN FRONT SUPPORT ONLY
$\frac{5}{8}$
5/16
$\frac{7}{8}$
6
$\frac{3}{8}$ DEEP
FRONT VIEW
$\frac{1}{16}$ DIA. HOLE - 4 PLACES

NO.	NAME	SIZE	REQ'D.
1	HEAD	5/8 X 4 – 8 1/2 LG.	1
2	JAW	5/8 X 1 1/4 – 5 LG.	1
3	CENTER BODY	5/8 X 5 – 5 1/2 LG.	1
4	TAIL	5/8 X 5 – 10 1/2 LG.	1
5	EYESCREW	SMALL SIZE	15
6	AXLE – REAR	1/8 DIA – 7 1/8 LG.	1
7	AXLE – FRONT	1/8 DIA – 8 1/4 LG.	1
8	DRIVE ROD	1/8 DIA. 7 1/2 LG.	1
9	AXLE SUPPORT	5/8 X 1 1/2 – 6 LG.	2
10	JAW HINGE	1/8 DIA. – 4 LONG	1
11	PIN	1/8 DIA. – 4 1/2 LG.	2
12	PULL LOOP	1/8 DIA. – 3 1/8 LG.	1
13	WHEEL	2 1/4 DIA. – 1/2 TK.	4

BEND ENDS AT 90° AT ASSEMBLY

NOTCH 5/8 WIDE - 5/16 DEEP
2 PLACES

NOTCH 5/8 WIDE - 5/16 DEEP
2 PLACES

BEND OVER
AT ASSEMBLY

NOTCH FRONT AXLE SUPPORT

EPOXY WHEELS ⑬ TO AXLES ⑥⑦

EXPLODED VIEW

♦11 Secure the drive rod to the jaw with a small eye screw. Experiment to find the best location for the eye screw.

♦12 Paint to suit. I have noted the colors and detailing that was on the original, if you want yours the same.

♦13 Assemble all parts using two pins, parts number 11. Bend them over at the top and bottom to hold them in place.

♦14 Epoxy the wheels, part number 13, to the axles, parts number 6 and 7.

♦15 Add the pull loop, part number 12, and your alligator is set to go.

21◆Elephant on Ball, circa 1945

This is a take-off of an elephant pull toy I saw in a photograph of toys of the 1940s and 1950s. The elephant rides up and down on the ball as the toy is pulled. Have fun with this one since you can make it as fancy as you wish. Circus wagons were always bright and gaudy.

Instructions

◆1   Cut all wood to basic size. Sand all over.

◆2   Make up the support structure, parts number 1 and 2, as shown. Drill the two ⁵⁄₁₆-inch-diameter holes for the axles. Sand all over.

◆3   On a 1-inch grid, lay out the side panel, part number 4, and transfer it to the wood and cut out. You will need two.

◆4   On a ½-inch grid, lay out the ball, elephant, legs, and ears. Transfer the patterns to the wood and cut out. Note that there are *two* parts number 12. Drill all holes.

◆5   Lay out the patterns for the front and back trim, parts number 5 and 6.

◆6   Glue the sides, parts number 4, to the support structure (Step 2).

◆7   Add the front, back, and center trim pieces, 5, 6, and 7, to the side, part number 4. (Continued on the following three pages.)

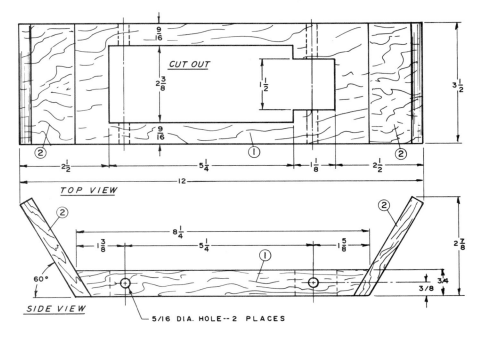

CUT OUT

TOP VIEW

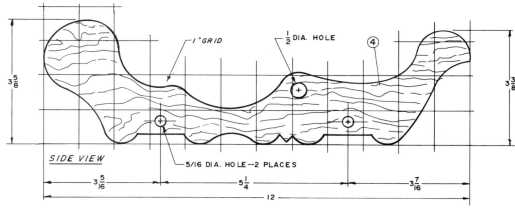

SIDE VIEW

5/16 DIA. HOLE--2 PLACES

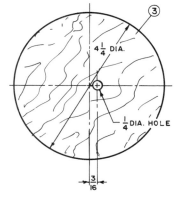

1" GRID

1/2 DIA. HOLE

SIDE VIEW

5/16 DIA. HOLE--2 PLACES

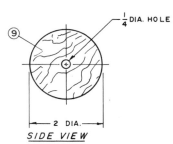

4 1/4 DIA.

1/4 DIA. HOLE

3/16

1/4 DIA. HOLE

2 DIA.

SIDE VIEW

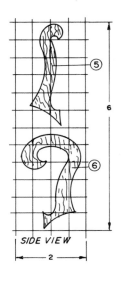

SIDE VIEW

NO.	NAME	SIZE	REQ'D.
1	BASE	3/4 X 3 1/2-8 1/4 LG.	1
2	END	3/8 X 3 1/2 - 3 5/16	2
3	DRIVE WHEEL	4 1/4 DIA. X 1/4 TK.	2
4	SIDE	3/8 X 3 5/8-12 LG.	2
5	TRIM - FRONT	1/8 X 1" - 3 LONG	2
6	TRIM-BACK	1/8 X 1 3/4-2 3/4 LG	2
7	TRIM-CENTER	1/8 X 5/16-2 5/8	2
8	AXLE-MAIN	1/4 DIA. X 2 1/2 LG.	1
9	WHEEL	2 DIA. X 5/8 TK.	4
10	FRONT AXLE	1/4 DIA. X 4 3/8 LG.	1
11	REAR PIN W/HEAD	1/4 DIA. X 1 1/2 LG.	2
12	BALL	3/4 X 3 1/2-5 1/4 LG.	2
13	BODY	3/4 X 5 - 7 1/2 LONG	1
14	REAR LEG	3/8 X 2 1/2 - 4 LONG	2
15	FRONT LEG	3/8 X 1 1/4 - 3 LG.	2
16	EAR	1/8 X 2 1/4 - 3 1/2 LG.	2
17	TUSK	1/8 X 1/2-1 1/4 LG.	2
18	EYESCREW	SMALL SIZE	1

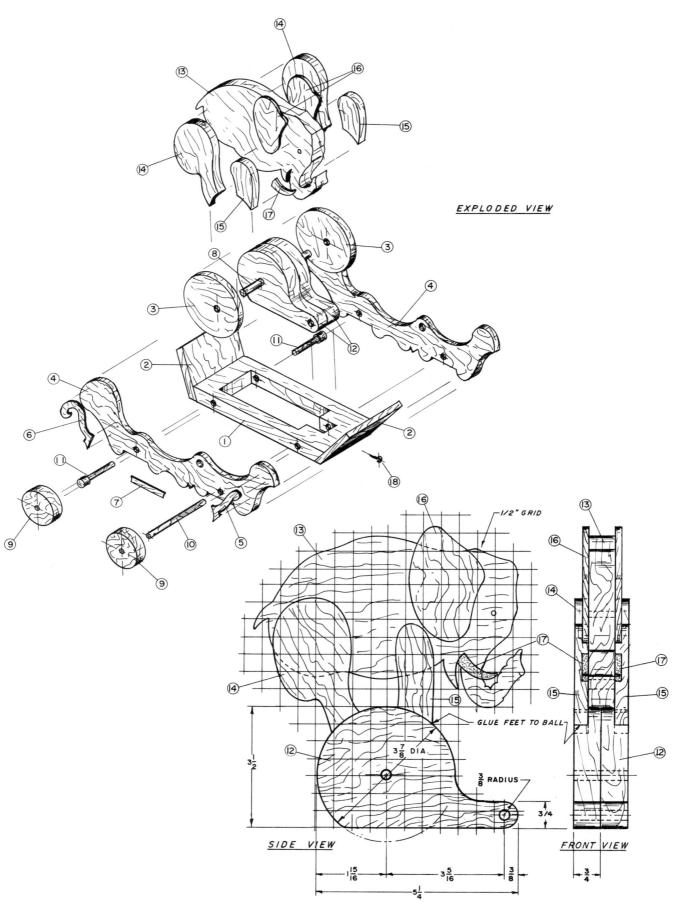

EXPLODED VIEW

1/2" GRID

GLUE FEET TO BALL

$3\frac{7}{8}$ DIA

$\frac{3}{8}$ RADIUS

$3\frac{1}{2}$

$\frac{3}{4}$

SIDE VIEW

$1\frac{15}{16}$

$3\frac{5}{16}$

$\frac{3}{8}$

$5\frac{1}{4}$

FRONT VIEW

$\frac{3}{4}$

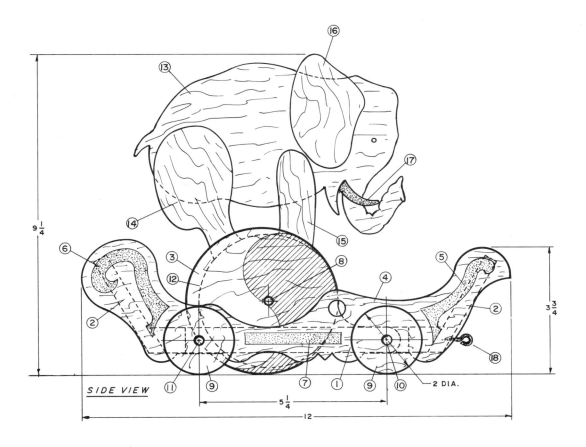

SIDE VIEW

♦8   Glue the elephant's legs, parts number 14 and 15, to the body, part number 13.

♦9   Add the ears, parts number 16, and the tusks, parts number 17, to the body.

♦10   Locate and glue the elephant assembly to the ball, parts number 12. (Locate as shown.)

♦11   Make the 4¼-inch-diameter drive wheels, parts number 3, as shown. Drill the ¼-inch-diameter holes ³/₁₆ inch off center. Sand all over.

♦12   Cut to size all axles and pins, parts number 8, 10, and 11.

♦13   Glue the drive wheels, parts number 3, to the axle, part number 8. Do not get any glue on the ball. Check that it turns freely.

♦14   Temporarily add the rear axle pins, parts number 11, and the front axle, part number 10, to the assembly. Add the wheels temporarily. Check that everything functions correctly.

♦15   Disassemble and paint with *bright*, nontoxic paint. Think "bright," using yellows, oranges, blues, and reds. Use your imagination and have fun.

♦16   Reassemble and add the eye screw, part number 18. You can almost hear the calliope.

22 ◆ Rattle on Wheels

This is a push toy that most tots just starting to walk will love. Paint it with bright colors, and it will really attract that three- or four-year-old.

Instructions

◆ 1 Cut all pieces to size according to the cutting list on page 75.

◆ 2 Lay out the two wheels and the twelve ³⁄₈-inch-diameter holes. Note that they are laid out on a 5-inch bolt circle and 30 degrees apart. (Refer to the side view.)

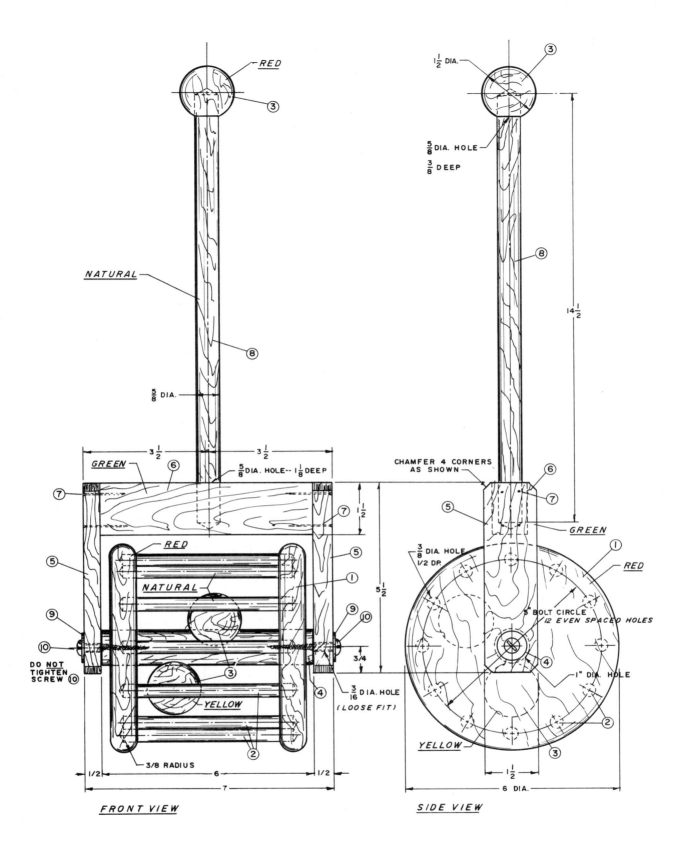

♦ 3 Cut out the two wheels, and drill the center 1-inch-diameter holes.

♦ 4 Round the outer edge of the wheels. Sand all over.

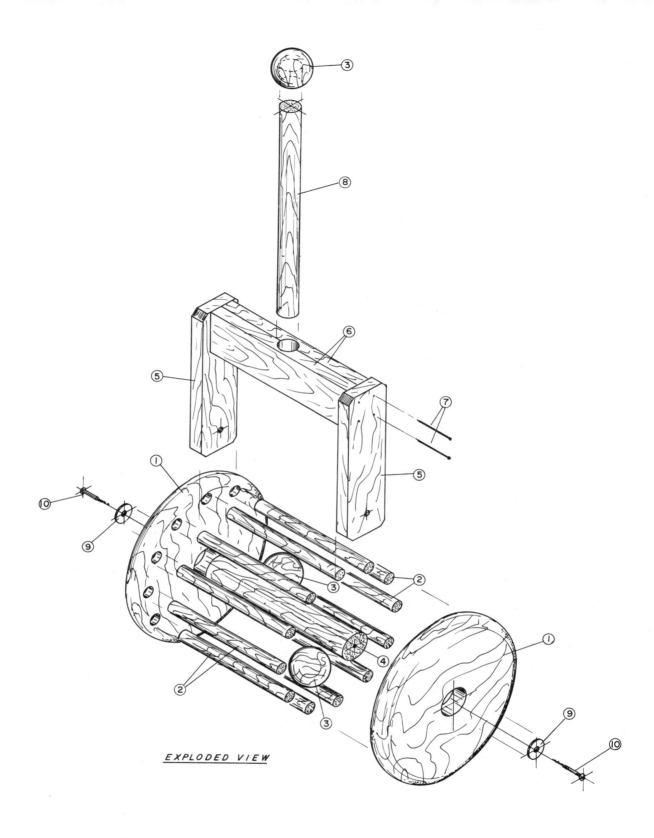

EXPLODED VIEW

♦5　Drill the twelve ⅜-inch-diameter holes in the wheel, ½ inch deep, as shown.

♦6　Cut all twelve bars, parts number 2, to length.

NO.	NAME	SIZE	REQ'D.
1	WHEEL	6 DIA. X 3/4 THICK	2
2	BAR	3/8 DIA. X 4 3/4 LG.	12
3	BALL	1 1/2 DIA.	3
4	AXLE	1" DIA. X 6 LONG	1
5	SUPPORT	1/2 X 1 1/2 - 5 1/2	2
6	SPACER	1/2 X 1 1/2 - 6 LONG	2
7	BRAD	1 1/4 LONG	8
8	HANDLE	5/8 DIA. X 14 1/2 LG.	1
9	WASHER	3/4 DIA.	2
10	SCREW — RD. HD.	NO. 8 X 2 LONG	2

♦7 *Temporarily* assemble the twleve bars to the wheels, and add the axle, part number 4. (The two balls can be left out at this time.)

♦8 Assemble the support, spacer, and handle, parts number 5, 6, and 8, according to the plans. Glue and nail them together.

♦9 Temporarily put together the handle assembly around the wheel assembly.

♦10 Check that everything turns freely.

♦11 Disassemble and paint all parts with bright, nontoxic paint.

♦12 Reassemble with glue. Make sure once more that the wheels turn freely. It's all set to go.

PUZZLES AND TRICKS

23 ◆ Monkey Business

This is a take-off of the old pipe-shaped belt trick. I simply made the old trick into a monkey. To use the balancing monkey, center and balance a regular belt in the tail, as shown. Balance the monkey on your finger or edge of a table at point "A."

Instructions

◆ 1   Transfer the monkey pattern to a piece of *high-grade* ¼-inch to ⁵⁄₁₆-inch-thick plywood. (Marine or aircraft plywood is best.)

$\frac{1}{4}"$ PLYWOOD

$5\frac{5}{8}$

BELT

FRONT VIEW

$4\frac{1}{8}$

TO USE:
PLACE A LEATHER BELT AS SHOWN ABOVE –
BALANCE MONKEY ON INDEX FINGER AT △

♦2   Carefully cut out, as shown.

♦3   Sand all over.

♦4   Paint the face, hands, and feet a light orange and the body dark brown or black.

♦5   Apply three or four coats of varnish to help strengthen the wood. Your monkey is ready to entertain you and your friends.

24◆Stegosaurus Puzzle

Dinosaurs are really big here in New Hampshire. My grandchildren have all kinds of dinosaur toys in all shapes, colors, and sizes. This is a simple puzzle that the very young will enjoy.

Instructions

◆1   On a 1-inch grid, lay out the pattern.

◆2   Transfer the pattern to the wood.

◆3   Cut the outside surfaces *first*, and slightly sand all edges.

◆4   Sand along the *bottom* of the feet so that the assembled puzzle will stand up.

3/4 THICK

1" GRID

7 3/8

16

SIDE VIEW

♦5 Paint to suit. Redraw the inner pieces.

♦6 Cut the inner pieces, as shown. If you stray *slightly* from the pattern, don't worry, no one will ever know.

♦7 Touch up all paint, as necessary.

25 ◆ Simple Square Puzzle

This puzzle looks easy. How hard can a four-piece puzzle be? Looks *are* deceiving; it's tougher than it looks. Be sure to paint each piece a *different* color, both sides and edges. (Suggested colors are given.)

Instructions

◆ 1 Sand all surfaces of a ¼-inch to ½-inch-thick piece of wood 5 inches square.

◆ 2 Carefully, lay out the pieces using the given design.

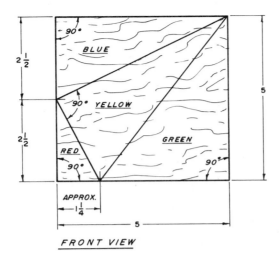

FRONT VIEW

♦3 Make the cuts for the pieces, using the *thinnest* saw blade you have.

♦4 Because of the saw blade thickness, the outer edges will have to be trimmed to make it square. (It will end up *slightly* smaller than the 5 inches square.)

♦5 Sand all over, surfaces and edges.

♦6 Apply one or two coats of primer, and sand lightly. (You want a nice smooth finish.)

♦7 Paint each piece a different color as noted.
Now the fun begins!

26♦Humpty Dumpty Puzzle

Do you remember what happened to Humpty Dumpty when he fell off the wall? Well, that is what happens to this Humpty Dumpty. It makes an interesting puzzle that children will enjoy putting back together—and love breaking into pieces again.

Instructions

♦1   On a piece of paper, lay out Humpty Dumpty and the wall, as shown.

♦2   Transfer the patterns to ¾-inch-thick wood. (The feet should be from ⅛-inch-thick wood.)

♦3   Cut out the main pieces, and sand all over. (Don't cut the puzzle pieces yet.)

♦4   I used a wood-burning tool and burnt in the bricks before painting. (This is optional.)

♦5   Paint your Humpty Dumpty as shown with bright, nontoxic paint.

♦6   Cut the body into the six pieces *after* painting.

♦7   Glue the two feet in place.
    That's it. Simple, huh?

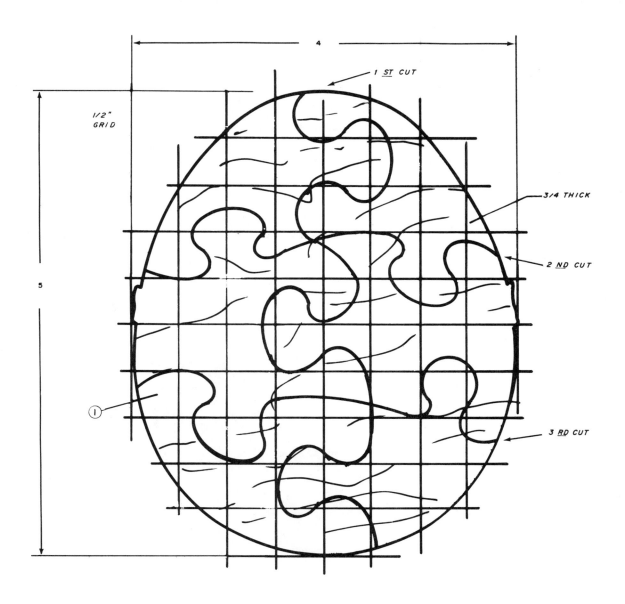

4

1 ST CUT

1/2" GRID

3/4 THICK

2 ND CUT

5

1

3 RD CUT

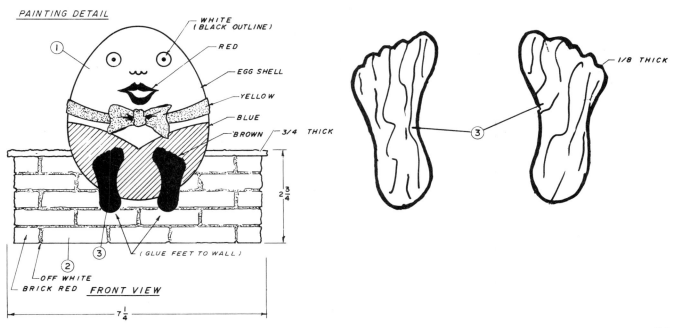

PAINTING DETAIL

WHITE
(BLACK OUTLINE)

RED

EGG SHELL

YELLOW

BLUE

BROWN — 3/4 THICK

1

3

2

OFF WHITE

BRICK RED

FRONT VIEW

(GLUE FEET TO WALL)

3¾

7¼

1/8 THICK

3

83

27♦Giraffe Puzzle

My grandchildren are fascinated with the giraffes whenever we visit a zoo. I think they spend more time with the giraffes than with the monkeys. Seeing they were so popular with them, I decided to make up a giraffe puzzle. Note: because of the long neck being off center, this puzzle, as drawn, will *not* stand up.

Instructions

♦1   Lay out a 1-inch grid, and transfer the shape to the grid as shown. (Include the pieces.)

♦2   Cut a piece of wood to size, ¾ inch by 7 inches, 15¾ inches long. Sand all over.

♦3   Apply a primer coat or two and sand all over so that you have a nice smooth finish.

♦4   Transfer the pattern *and* pieces to the wood.

♦5   Cut out each piece.

♦6   Paint each piece a different color. Your giraffe is finished.

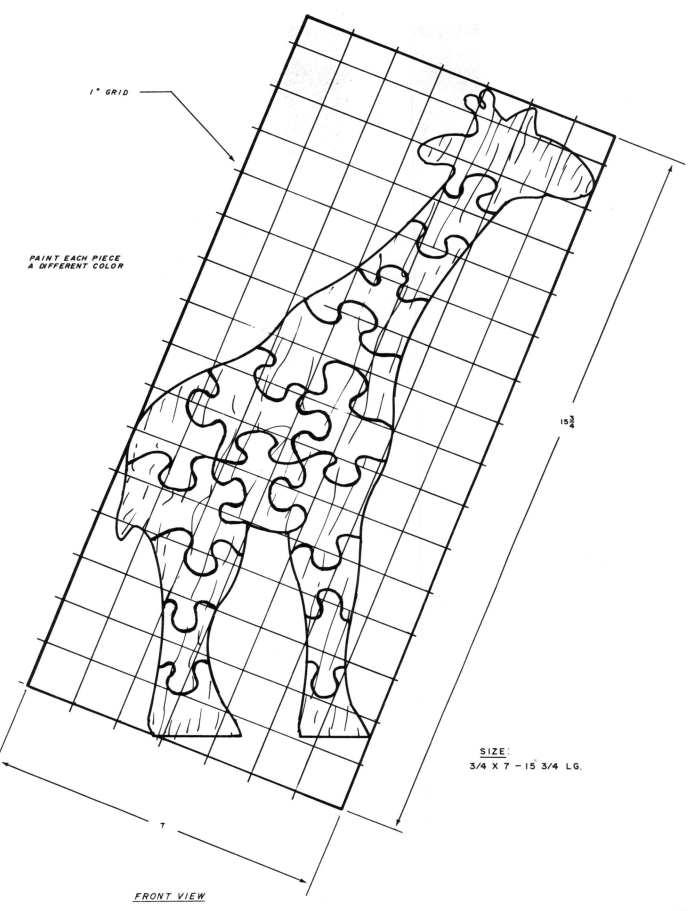

1" GRID

PAINT EACH PIECE
A DIFFERENT COLOR

$15\frac{3}{4}$

SIZE:
3/4 X 7 — 15 3/4 LG.

7

FRONT VIEW

28 ◆ Color/Shape Puzzle

This toy teaches counting, color, *and* shape. It is especially good for two-to three-year-old children.

Instructions

◆1   Cut pieces to overall sizes according to the cutting list.

◆2   Sand the back, part number 2.

◆3   On the top board, part number 1, carefully lay out the three overall cutouts using the given dimensions (top view).

◆4   Cut out the three holes and glue the top board, part number 1, to the back, part number 2.

◆5   After the glue dries, sand all surfaces and edges.

◆6   Using a "rounding" router bit with a ball-bearing follower, round the edges, as shown.

◆7   On ¾-inch- or 1-inch-thick material, lay out the triangle, circle, and square.

◆8   Cut out the three pieces, and "round" all edges. Sand all over.

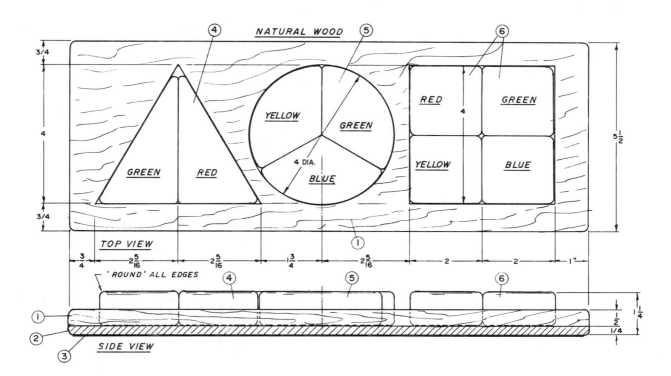

NO.	NAME	SIZE	REQ'D.
1	TOP BOARD	1/2 X 5 1/2 - 14 1/2	1
2	BACK	1/4 X 5 1/2 - 14 1/2	1
3	FELT (OPTIONAL)	5 1/4 X 14 1/4	1
4	TRIANGLE	1 X 4 - 4 1/2 LG.	1
5	CIRCLE	1 X 4 DIA.	1
6	SQUARE	1 X 4 SQUARE	1

NOTE: PARTS ④⑤⑥ COULD BE 3/4 THICK

♦9   Cut the triangle in two pieces, the circle in three pieces, and the square in four pieces.

♦10   Sand all pieces.

♦11   Prime and paint with bright colors, using nontoxic paint. Your two- or three-year-old will really love this puzzle!

29◆Photograph Puzzle, 8 Inch by 10 Inch

Puzzles are always fun to make and fun to solve. By using a photograph, you can make your puzzle very "personal."

Instructions

◆1 Have an 8-inch by 10-inch enlargement made of your favorite photograph.

◆2 Cut a ¼-inch- or ⅜-inch-thick piece of *high-grade* plywood (marine or aircraft) to 8 inches by 10 inches.

◆3 Sand both surfaces smooth, and sand all edges.

◆4 Apply two to three coats of varnish to all surfaces, and sand smooth.

◆5 Using rubber cement or a spray-mount adhesive, attach the photograph to the top surface. Apply adhesive to the back of the photograph and to the top surface. Let dry. Carefully attach photo to the wood after the adhesive dries.

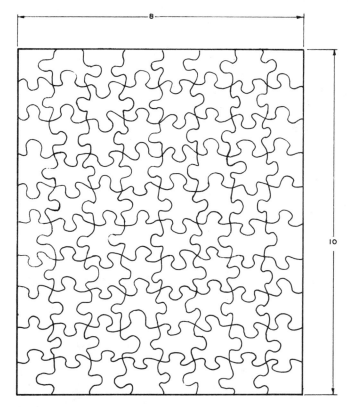

TOP VIEW

♦6 Glue a blank piece of heavy paper to the bottom surface to protect the wood from splintering when you cut out the pattern.

♦7 Carefully sand all four edges.

♦8 Apply a coat of varnish to the edges and over the heavy paper on the back.

♦9 Enlarge the pattern of the individual pieces to 8 inches by 10 inches.

♦10 Using a *light* coat of rubber cement or spray-mount adhesive on the back of the pattern, apply the pattern directly over the photograph. Do not press down too much; you only want the pattern to stay in place while you are cutting out the pieces.

♦11 Using a very fine blade, make all *top-to-bottom* cuts. *Try* to stay on the lines, but if you're off a *little* it won't matter.

♦12. Temporarily tape the eight strips together from the back using masking tape.

♦13 Make all horizontal side-to-side cuts.

♦14 Remove all masking tape, and carefully remove the paper pattern from the photograph. Your personal puzzle is completed, all 80 pieces.

FOLK ART TOYS

30 ◆ Tic-Tac-Toe Game

Here is an old favorite. I especially like this project because it makes a great gift, and it can be made from the scraps from the other projects in this book.

Instructions

◆1 Cut the case from a piece of scrap wood, 1 inch by 4½ inches by 4½ inches. Sand all over.

◆2 Carefully make the four saw kerfs, as shown. Resand all over.

◆3 Drill the two ⅝-inch-diameter holes for the marbles in one side, 2¾ inches deep, as shown.

◆4 Using a drill "stop," locate and make the nine ⅝-inch-diameter indentations. Make all of them the same depth: approximately ⅛ inch deep.

◆5 Make the lid to cover the holes in the side according to given dimensions.

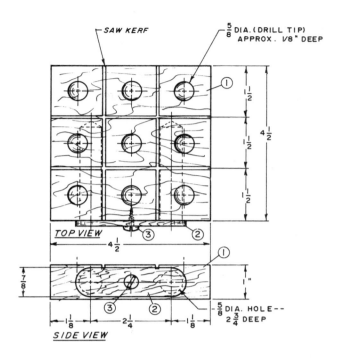

SAW KERF

⁵⁄₈ DIA. (DRILL TIP)
APPROX. 1/8" DEEP

1½

4½

1½

1½

TOP VIEW

4½

⅞

1"

1/8   2¼   1/8

⁵⁄₈ DIA. HOLE --
2¾ DEEP

SIDE VIEW

NO.	NAME	SIZE	REQ'D.
1	CASE	1 X 4 1/2 - 4 1/2 LG.	1
2	LID	1/8 X 7/8 - 3 1/8 LG.	1
3	SCREW-RD. HD.	NO. 6 - 1" LONG	2
4	MARBLE	1/2 DIA.	8

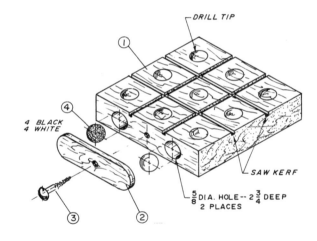

DRILL TIP

4 BLACK
4 WHITE

⁵⁄₈ DIA. HOLE -- 2¾ DEEP
2 PLACES

SAW KERF

EXPLODED VIEW

♦6   Sand all over, and paint or varnish the pieces to suit. You might want to add *color* to the nine indentations.

♦7   Assemble the pieces using either a roundhead or flathead screw.

♦8   Be sure to use ½-inch-diameter marbles. Use four of two different colors, such as four white, four black. Let the game begin!

31 ◆ "Push" Chicken

I found this neat old toy in an antique shop. I would guess it is about 50 years old—a toy the kids will love.

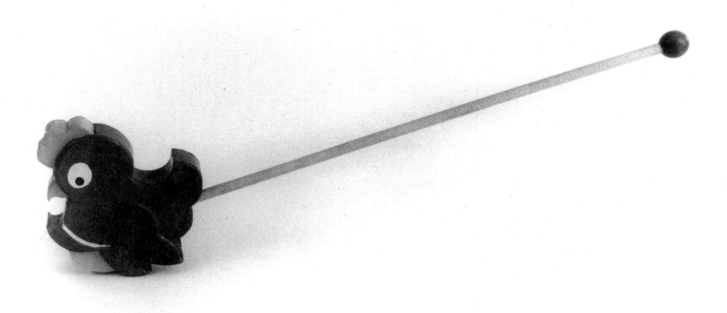

Instructions

◆1   Cut all parts to overall size.

◆2   On a ½-inch grid, lay out the pieces, parts number 1, 2, and 3.

◆3   Carefully cut out, and sand all over.

◆4   Carefully locate and drill the ¼-inch-diameter holes in the sides, parts number 2.

◆5   Drill the ⅜-inch-diameter hole in the body center, part number 1, at 45 degrees, as shown, and 1½ inches deep.

◆6   Assemble all pieces according to the exploded view. Check that the wheel turns freely. Be sure to add the wheel before assembling the sides since the wheel will not fit in after assembly.

◆7   Paint with bright, nontoxic colors. (I have noted the colors used on the original.)

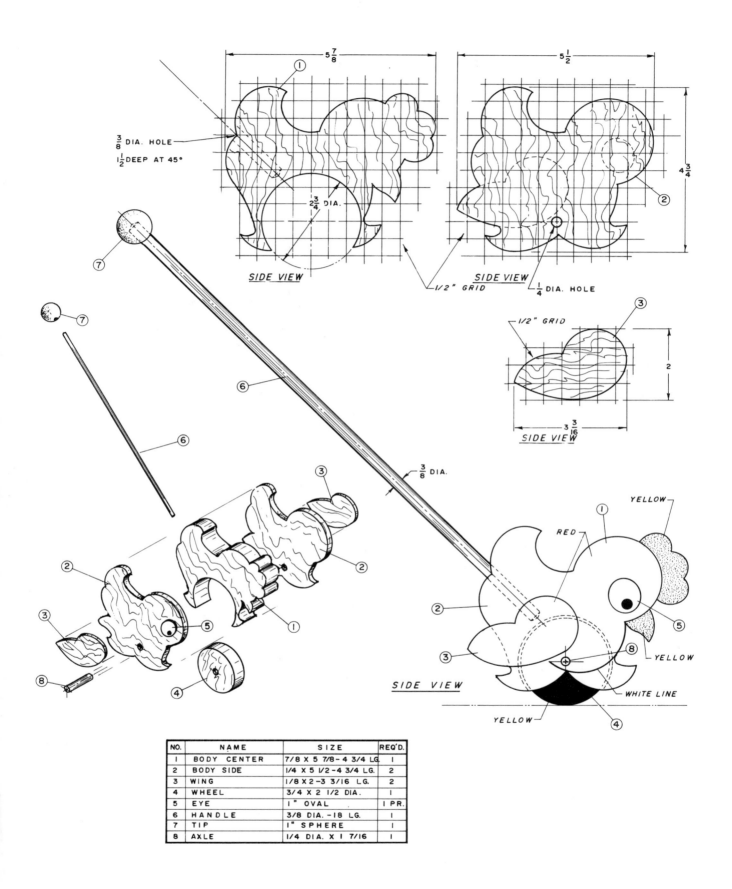

NO.	NAME	SIZE	REQ'D.
1	BODY CENTER	7/8 X 5 7/8 – 4 3/4 LG.	1
2	BODY SIDE	1/4 X 5 1/2 – 4 3/4 LG.	2
3	WING	1/8 X 2 – 3 3/16 LG.	2
4	WHEEL	3/4 X 2 1/2 DIA.	1
5	EYE	1" OVAL	1 PR.
6	HANDLE	3/8 DIA. – 18 LG.	1
7	TIP	1" SPHERE	1
8	AXLE	1/4 DIA. X 1 7/16	1

Note: The oval eyes, parts number 5, should be painted on if the toy is
for a very small child.

32 ♦ Cow Jumping over Moon

This simple toy gives life to the poem "Hey diddle, diddle, the cat and the fiddle, and the cow jumped over the moon." It makes an interesting toy.

Instructions

♦ 1   Transfer the shapes of the cow, moon, and base to ¾-inch-thick wood.

♦ 2   Cut out the cow, moon, and base, and sand all over.

♦ 3   Drill ¼-inch-diameter holes in the base, cow, and moon, as shown.

♦ 4   Assemble with ¼-inch-diameter dowel cut to the lengths indicated. Paint to suit.

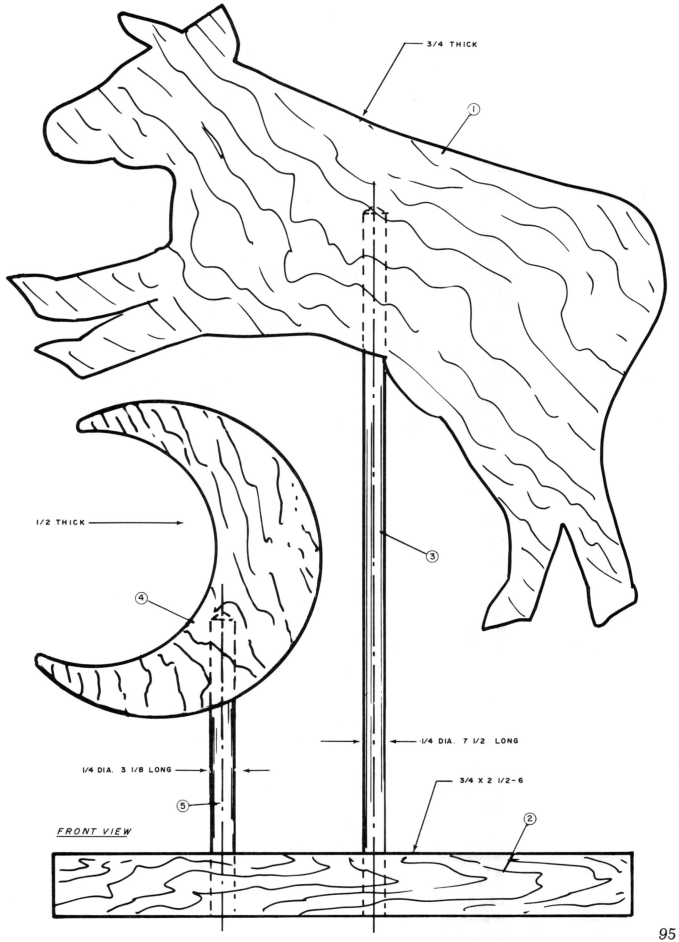

3/4 THICK

①

1/2 THICK

③

④

-1/4 DIA. 7 1/2 LONG

1/4 DIA. 3 1/8 LONG

3/4 X 2 1/2-6

⑤

②

FRONT VIEW

95

33 ◆ Rabbit with Cart

This project is a copy of an original toy made around 1940. It makes a great Easter basket. The bunny hops along as it is pushed.

Instructions

◆1 Cut all pieces to size according to the cutting list.

◆2 On a ½-inch grid, lay out the body, part number 1, and base, part number 2. Transfer the patterns to the wood and cut out. Sand all over.

◆3 Using the exploded view as a guide, assemble the cart using parts number 2 through 10.

◆4 Form the rear axle, part number 10, as shown.

◆5 *Temporarily* add the rabbit, part number 1, and connecting parts 11 through 15. Check that everything works correctly.

◆6 Disassemble and paint following the suggested colors or your own color scheme.

◆7 Reassemble, and check that everything functions correctly.
    Note: The wheels should be glued to the axles, preferably with epoxy.

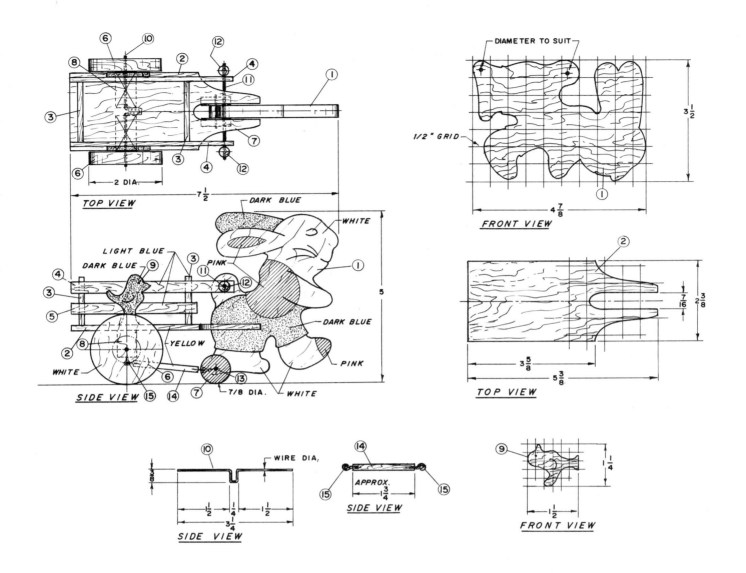

NO.	NAME	SIZE	REQ'D.
1	BODY	3/8 X 3 1/2 - 4 7/8 LG.	1
2	BASE	3/16 X 2 3/8 - 5 3/8 LG.	1
3	END RAIL	3/16 X 1 7/16 - 1 3/4 LG	2
4	TOP RAIL	3/16 X 3/8 - 4 5/8 LG.	2
5	BOTTOM RAIL	3/16 X 3/8 - 3 9/16	2
6	WHEEL BACK	3/8 X 2 DIA.	2
7	WHEEL FRONT	1/4 X 7/8 DIA.	2
8	AXLE SUPPORT	1/2 X 3/4 - 1 LONG	2
9	BIRD	1/8 X 1 1/4 - 1 1/2 LG.	2
10	AXLE - REAR	WIRE DIA. X 4 1/8 LG.	1
11	PIN - PIVOT	WIRE DIA. X 2 3/4 LG.	1
12	SPHERE	5/16 DIA.	2
13	AXLE - FRONT	WIRE DIA. X 1 LG.	1
14	CONNECTING ROD	1/4 X 1/4 - 1 3/4 LG.	1
15	EYE SCREW	SMALL	4

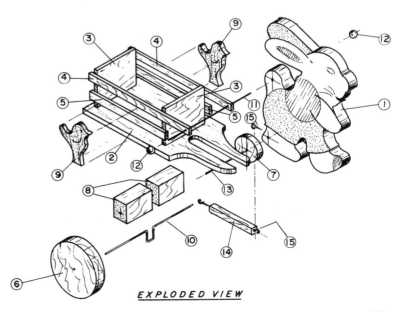

EXPLODED VIEW

34 ◆ Small Rocking Horse

I feel that all children should have a rocking horse. This one is a little small but nevertheless a rocking horse. It is fun to make and paint, as well as to play with.

Instructions

◆1   Lay out the horse and rocker on a ½-inch grid. Note that it could be made *twice* the size if you lay it out on a 1-inch grid.

◆2   Cut all pieces to overall size according to the cutting list. Sand all over.

◆3   Transfer the shapes of the horse, legs, and rocker to the wood and cut out. Sand all pieces, rounding all edges slightly.

◆4   Assemble the rocker section first, parts number 6 and 7. Keep the rockers parallel to each other.

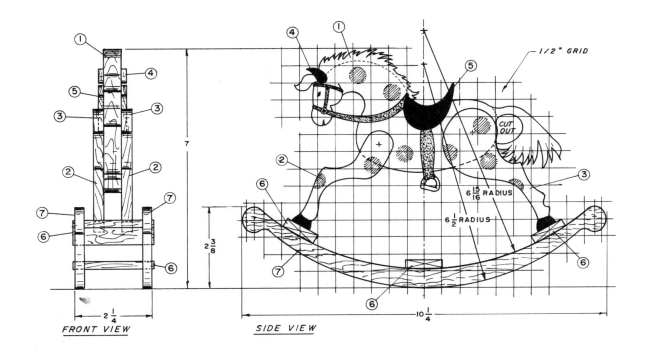

FRONT VIEW

SIDE VIEW

NO.	NAME	SIZE	REQ'D.
1	BODY	1/2 X 3 5/8 – 8 LG.	1
2	FRONT LEG	1/4 X 1 1/2 – 4 LG.	2
3	BACK	1/4 X 2 – 4 1/4 LG.	2
4	EAR	1/8 X 3/8 – 3/4 LG	2
5	SADDLE	1/8 X 1 1/4 – 2 LONG	1
6	SUPPORT	1/4 X 1 – 1 3/8 LONG	3
7	ROCKER	1/4 X 2 1/2 – 10 1/2	2

Note: If you expect hard use, you might want to consider gluing *and* nailing the pieces together.

♦ **5** Glue the legs to both the horse's body *and* the rocker assembly at the same time. This will ensure correct alignment of the legs, parts number 2 and 3, with the supports, parts number 6. (It also takes three hands to do it!)

♦ **6** Prime the toy. You *might* consider staining the rockers, parts number 7.

♦ **7** Now comes the fun part; paint and decorate your horse as you wish. Use your imagination and have fun!

35◆Model "T" Truck

This is a toy that teaches both history and thrift. It is a 1925 Model "T" Ford truck. The Model "T" Ford was made from 1909 through 1927 and single-handedly put America on wheels. It teaches thrift because it is a *bank*.

Instructions

◆1   Cut all pieces to overall size according to the cutting list.

◆2   On a ½-inch grid, lay out all pieces. Take care that the *outer* shape of the body, parts number 1 and 2, are exactly the same.

◆3   Cut the *interior* of the center, part number 1. Locate and cut the slot, as shown.

◆4   Cut out the window on the two sides, parts number 2.

◆5   Glue the *two* sides, parts number 2, over the center section, and cut out the *outer* edges of the car.

◆6   Locate and drill the two ¼-inch-diameter holes for the axles.

◆7   Sand all over.

◆8   Add the hood, part number 6, and radiator, part number 7, in place.

◆9   Cut out the fenders, parts number 3. Be sure to make a right and left *matched* pair of fenders. (Continued on the following three pages.)

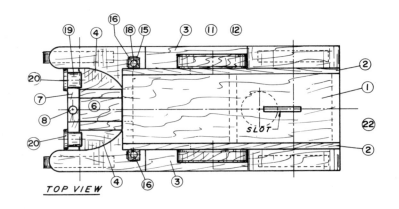

TOP VIEW

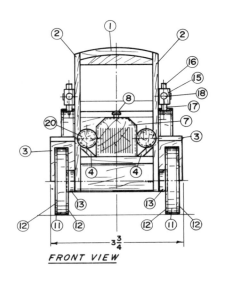

FRONT VIEW

$3\frac{3}{4}$

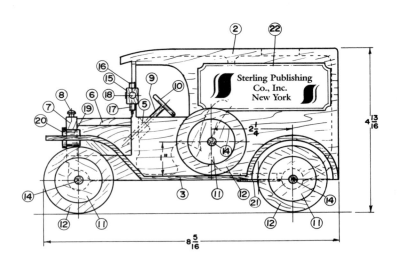

Sterling Publishing Co., Inc. New York

$4\frac{13}{16}$

$2\frac{1}{4}$

$8\frac{5}{16}$

NO.	NAME	SIZE	REQ'D.
1	CENTER	2 X 4 1/4 - 7 3/4 LG.	1
2	SIDE	3/16 X 4 1/4 - 7 3/4	2
3	FENDER	1 1/4 X 1 5/16-8 1/4	2
4	FILLER	1/8 X 1 - 1 3/8 LG.	2
5	SUPPORT-COLUMN	1/2 X 1/2 -1/2 LG	1
6	HOOD	1 1/16 X 1 1/8 - 1 1/2	1
7	RADIATOR	5/16 X 1 1/8 - 1 1/4	1
8	CAP	3/16 DIA.-7/16 LG.	1
9	COLUMN	1/8 DIA.-1 1/4 LG.	1
10	WHEEL	7/8 DIA.-1/8 LG.	1
11	TIRE	1/16 X 2 SQUARE	12
12	RIM	1/4 X 2 SQUARE	6
13	SPACER	5/8 DIA. X 3/16 LG.	4
14	AXLE PEG		6
15	PARKING LAMP	5/16 X 5/16-1/2 LG.	2
16	TOP	3/16 DIA. X 5/16 LG.	2
17	BOTTOM	3/16 DIA.X 3/8 LG.	2
18	LENSE	3/16 DIA. X 1/8 LG.	4
19	BODY	1/2 DIA. X 3/8 LG.	2
20	LENSE	5/8 DIA.X 1/8 LG.	2
21	STOPPER		1
22	SIGN (TO SUIT)	1 3/8 X 3 3/4 LG.	2

♦10 Fit the filler, parts number 4, to the fenders, parts number 3, as shown.

♦11 Fit the fenders to the body, and glue in place.

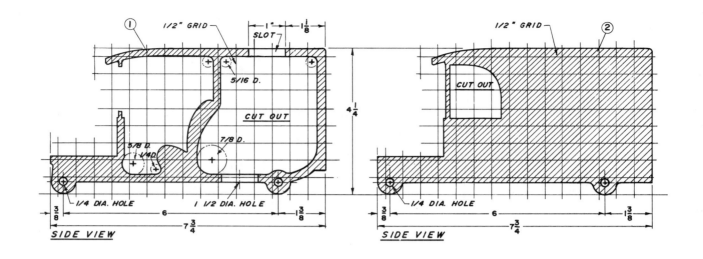

① ½" GRID   1" 1⅛
SLOT
5/16 D.
CUT OUT
4¼
5/8 D.
7/8 D.
¼ D.
¼ DIA. HOLE   1½ DIA. HOLE
3/8   6   1⅜
7¾
SIDE VIEW

② ½" GRID
CUT OUT
¼ DIA. HOLE
3/8   6   1⅜
7¾
SIDE VIEW

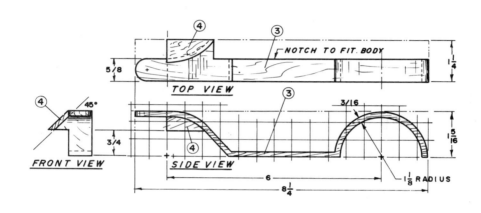

④   ③ NOTCH TO FIT BODY   1¼
5/8
TOP VIEW

④ 45°   ③   3/16
3/4   ④   1 5/16
SIDE VIEW   1⅛ RADIUS
6
8¼
FRONT VIEW

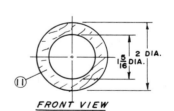
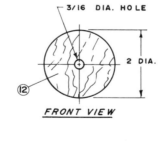

3/16 DIA. HOLE
2 DIA.
⑫
FRONT VIEW

2 DIA.
1 5/16 DIA.
⑪
FRONT VIEW

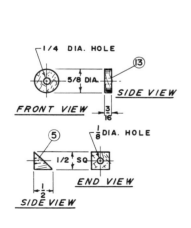

¼ DIA. HOLE
5/8 DIA.   ⑬
SIDE VIEW
3/16
FRONT VIEW

⑤   ⅛ DIA. HOLE
½ SQ
½
END VIEW
SIDE VIEW

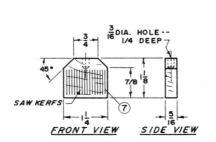

3/4   3/16 DIA. HOLE --
¼ DEEP
45°   7/8   1⅛
SAW KERFS   1¼   5/16
⑦
FRONT VIEW   SIDE VIEW

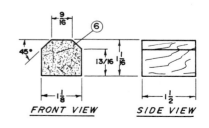

9/16   ⑥
45°   13/16   1 1/16
1⅛   1½
FRONT VIEW   SIDE VIEW

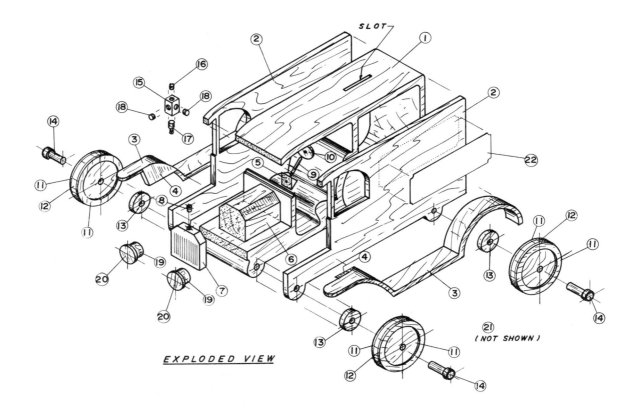

SLOT

EXPLODED VIEW

♦12   Assemble all other miscellaneous pieces according to the exploded view.

♦13   Make up wheels by gluing the tires, parts number 11, to the wheels, parts number 10. (See the exploded view.)

♦14   Temporarily add the wheels to the body. Check that everything fits correctly.

♦15   Paint all over to suit.

♦16.   Add wheels and axles. Your Model "T" is ready for the road.

36 ♦ Jumping Clown, circa 1940

This project will really give you a chance to "clown" around. As you squeeze the handle, the clown jumps and twirls. It is a take-off of a very old toy that has been around for over 100 years. You can make various jumping clowns, or acrobats, or animals by simply changing the body and arms slightly.

Instructions

♦1 Cut all wood to approximate size according to the cutting list. I recommend that the handle and spacer parts be made of a straight-grained hardwood. The body and arms can be made out of softwood.

♦2 Assemble the handle, parts number 1, and spacer, part number 2, with small tacks or brads, parts number 3. (Do *not* glue.) You might want to drill small holes first so the wood does not split.

♦3 Lay out and cut out the body and arms.

♦4 Drill holes in the handles, parts number 1, body, part number 4, and arms and legs, parts number 5 and 6.

♦5 Sand all over.

♦6 Paint to suit; use your imagination.

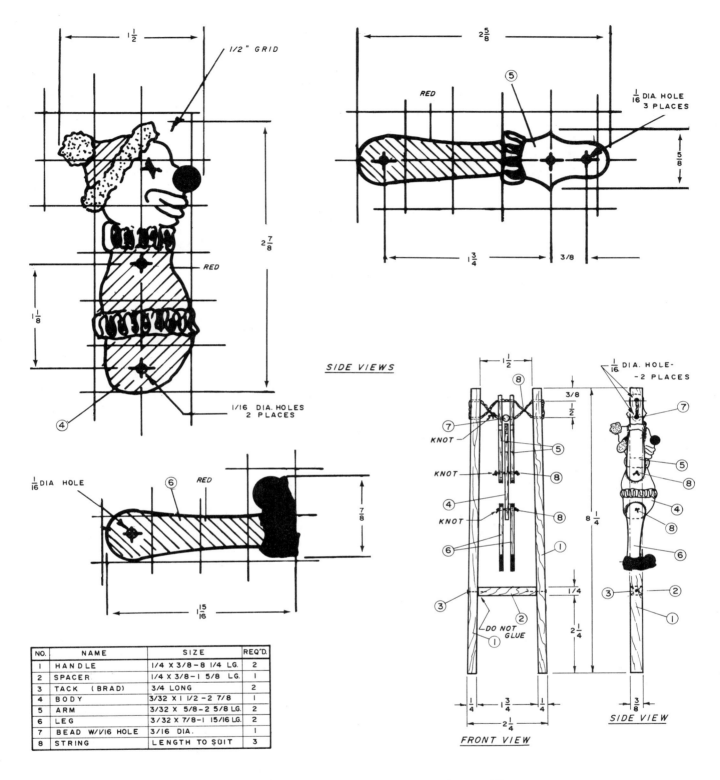

SIDE VIEWS

NO.	NAME	SIZE	REQ'D.
I	HANDLE	1/4 X 3/8 - 8 1/4 LG.	2
2	SPACER	1/4 X 3/8 - 1 5/8 LG.	I
3	TACK (BRAD)	3/4 LONG	2
4	BODY	3/32 X 1 1/2 - 2 7/8	I
5	ARM	3/32 X 5/8 - 2 5/8 LG.	2
6	LEG	3/32 X 7/8 - 1 15/16 LG.	2
7	BEAD W/1/16 HOLE	3/16 DIA.	I
8	STRING	LENGTH TO SUIT	3

FRONT VIEW

SIDE VIEW

♦7   Assemble the arms and legs to the body with string, as shown. Keep it all loose.

♦8   Assemble the arms to the handles, as shown. Be sure to use a bead with a hole, part number 7, or some kind of a small spacer. Thread the string as shown in the *front view*.

♦9   Check that the clown will jump when the handles are squeezed. Adjust, as necessary.

37◆Noisemaker, circa 1940

As a parent you will probably *hate* this project. As a grandparent, I think it is *great*! (I don't have to listen to it all day.) This is a copy of a noisemaker I saw in an antique shop in North Hampton, New Hampshire. It was made of maple and made a *lot* of noise.

Instructions

◆1   Cut all pieces to size out of hardwood.

◆2   Glue the two blocks, parts number 2, to the clicker, part number 3. Be sure to step the clicker down about 3/32 of an inch or so, as shown, so that it does not touch the top or bottom, parts number 1.

◆3   Glue the two blocks and clicker to the top and bottom, as shown.

◆4   Locate and drill a 3/8-inch-diameter hole through the top and bottom.

◆5   Turn the handle according to the given dimensions. Especially check the 3/8-inch-diameter shank.

◆6   Lay out and cut the ratchet, part number 6, as shown. Drill the 3/8-inch-diameter hole.

◆7   Finish all parts with a varnish or some clear coat of material.

◆8   Assemble by attaching the handle, part number 4, up through the top and bottom, parts number 1, and into the ratchet. Check that the clicker clears the ratchet correctly. (Continued on the following two pages.)

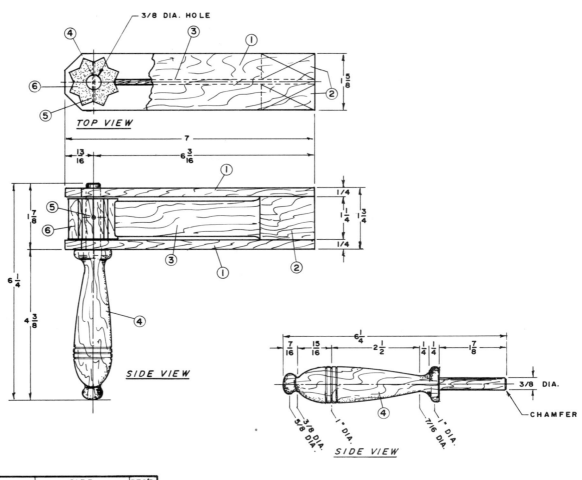

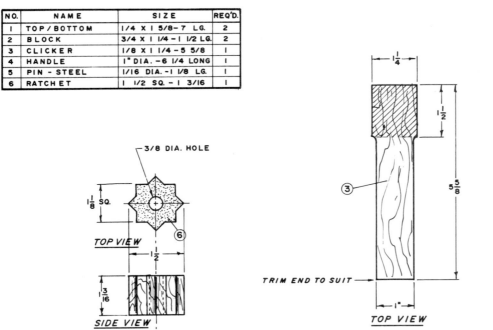

NO.	NAME	SIZE	REQ'D.
1	TOP / BOTTOM	1/4 X 1 5/8 - 7 LG.	2
2	BLOCK	3/4 X 1 1/4 - 1 1/2 LG.	2
3	CLICKER	1/8 X 1 1/4 - 5 5/8	1
4	HANDLE	1" DIA. - 6 1/4 LONG	1
5	PIN - STEEL	1/16 DIA. - 1 1/8 LG.	1
6	RATCHET	1 1/2 SQ. - 1 3/16	1

Note: The clicker *might* have to be thinned down from ⅛ inch thick. Experiment, since different wood will respond differently.

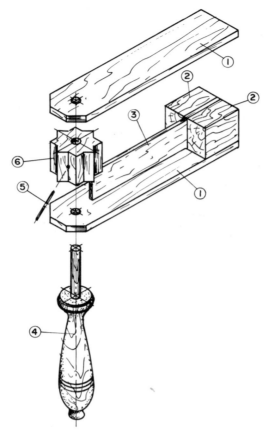

EXPLODED VIEW

♦ 9   If all works okay, pin everything together with part number 5.

♦ 10   Check that it makes a good strong sound. Enjoy!

38 ◆ Piggy Bank

Having raised pigs in northern Vermont years ago, I really appreciate them. They are very smart, fun to have around, and believe it or not a very clean animal. This is a pig that you can take to the bank. Perhaps, if you're lucky, this project may instill thrift into your little ones.

Instructions

◆1   Cut all parts to overall size, and sand the top and bottom surfaces.

◆2   Lay out the pieces on a 1-inch grid.
   Note: There are five pieces that make up the body; two ¾ inch thick, two ½ inch thick, and one ¼ inch thick. Don't forget to lay out the *interior* cut for the center pieces, 2 and 3.

◆3   Transfer the patterns to the wood.

◆4   Cut out the *center* areas of the three center pieces, 2 and 3. Cut the tail in part 3 only.

◆5   Line up all pieces *except* the center piece, part number 3, and cut away the wood where the tail would be. (Tail is only on center piece.) (Continued on the following two pages.)

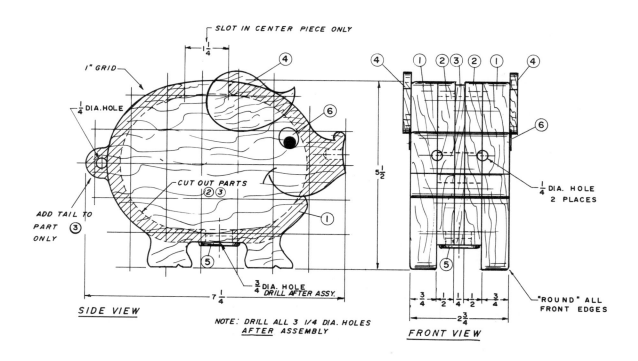

NO.	NAME	SIZE	REQ'D.
1	BODY / LEGS	3/4 X 5 1/2 - 6 3/4	2
2	CENTER	1/2 X 4 3/4 - 7 1/4	2
3	CENTER/SLOT	1/4 X 4 3/4 - 7 1/4	1
4	EAR	1/8 X 1 3/4 - 2 1/2	2
5	PLUG	3/4 DIA.	1
6	EYE (OVAL)	5/8 SIZE	2

♦6   Line up the three center pieces, 2 and 3, and cut away the wood where the legs would be.

♦7   Line up *all* of the pieces and glue them together.

♦8   Make the rest of the outer body cutout starting and ending in the tail section. (Don't forget to leave the tail on the center section and the legs on the two *outer* pieces.)

♦9   Drill ¼-inch-diameter holes in the tail and nose.

♦10   Drill a ¾-inch-diameter hole up from the bottom for the plug.

♦11   Sand all over and "round" all edges slightly. (I used a ⅛-inch-radius router bit with a ball-bearing follower.)

♦12   Cut out and add the ears, parts number 4, as shown.

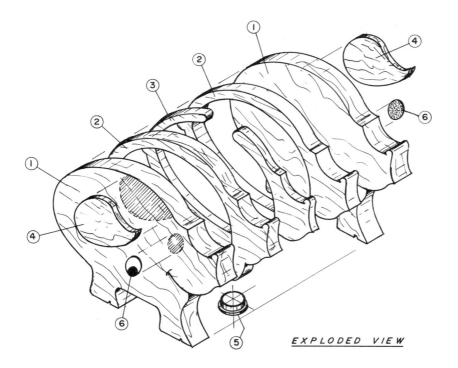

EXPLODED VIEW

♦ 13 The eyes can either be painted on or you can use ⅝-inch-diameter jiggling eyes that glue on. If small children might get their hands on this piggy bank, only use paint for the eyes.

♦ 14 Add a plug—either a made-up plug or purchased rubber plug.

♦ 15 Paint to suit. I especially like a pink pig. Add a new penny for luck!

39♦Hobbyhorse, circa 1890

We lived on a farm in northern Vermont when my daughters were young. They had to have a *real* horse. Here is a horse *I* really like. You don't have to house it, feed it, or pasture it. It doesn't need a lot of room or have to have new shoes every spring. Your live-in cowboy or cowgirl will love this horse—and you will too!

Instructions

♦1 Cut all pieces to overall size.

♦2 On a 1-inch grid, lay out the head. Include the locations of the two ¾-inch-diameter holes.

♦3 Transfer the pattern to the wood.

♦4 Glue up two ½-inch-thick pieces, if you don't have any 1-inch-thick material.

♦5 Cut out the pattern.

♦6 Cut the two side pieces, parts number 2.

♦7 Sand all pieces; "round" edges slightly.

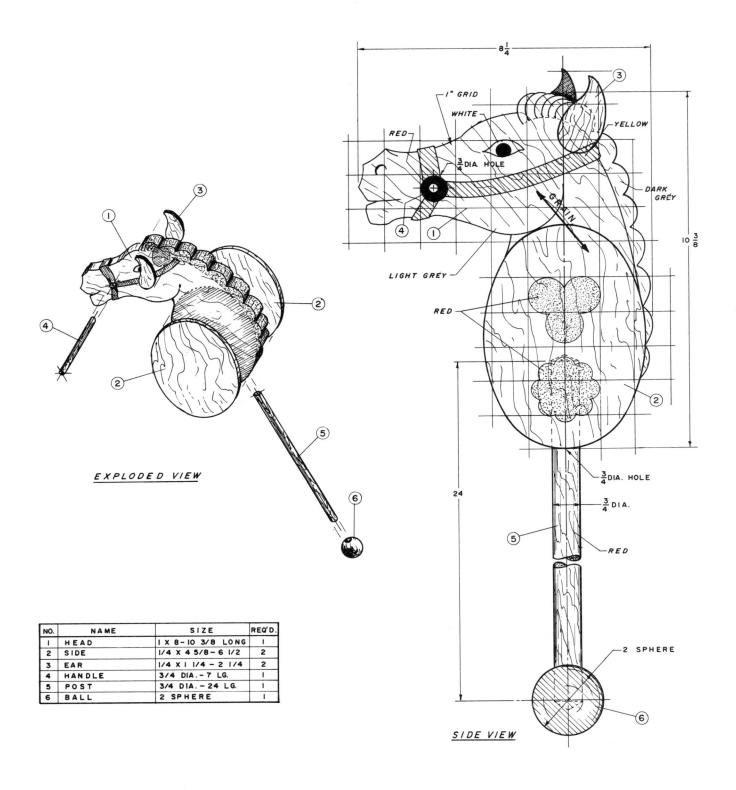

EXPLODED VIEW

SIDE VIEW

NO.	NAME	SIZE	REQ'D.
1	HEAD	1 X 8 - 10 3/8 LONG	1
2	SIDE	1/4 X 4 5/8 - 6 1/2	2
3	EAR	1/4 X 1 1/4 - 2 1/4	2
4	HANDLE	3/4 DIA. - 7 LG.	1
5	POST	3/4 DIA. - 24 LG.	1
6	BALL	2 SPHERE	1

♦8   Glue the side pieces, parts number 2, to the head, part number 1.

♦9   Locate and drill the two ¾-inch-diameter holes.

♦10   Add the handle, part number 4, the post, part number 5, and ball, part number 6.

♦11   Paint to suit. This is a copy of an old English hobbyhorse, and the suggested design is from that original. Use bright colors.

40♦Elephant Stool

This project is both a stool and a small chair. It has hand holes so your child or grandchild can easily carry it around. It is great for helping them into things they shouldn't get into!

Instructions

♦1   Cut wood to overall size. (The body pieces are designed to be made from a one-by-ten piece of wood.)

♦2   On a 1-inch grid, lay out the body. Note the location of the braces, parts number 2, on the pattern.

♦3   Transfer the pattern to the wood and cut out. (Cut both body pieces together.)

♦4   Sand all over. Slightly round all edges.

♦5   Assemble according to the exploded view.

♦6   Paint to suit.

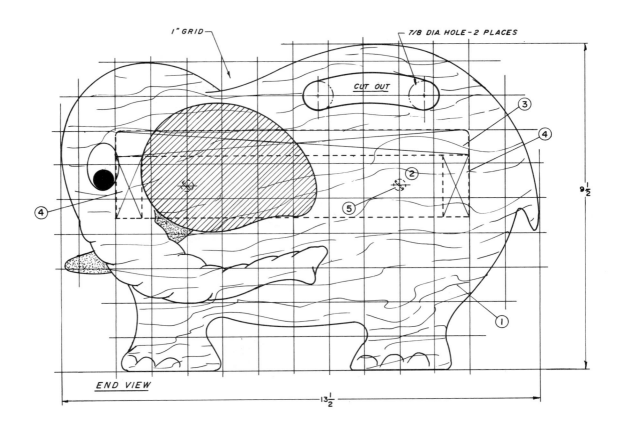

1" GRID

7/8 DIA. HOLE - 2 PLACES

CUT OUT

③

④

②

⑤

④

①

9½

13½

END VIEW

NO.	NAME	SIZE	REQ'D.
1	BODY	3/4 X 9 1/2 –13 1/2	2
2	BRACE	3/4 X 1 3/4 – 8 LG.	2
3	SEAT	3/4 X 9 1/2 –12 LG.	1
4	SKIRT	3/4 X 1 3/4 –12 LG.	2
5	SCREW – FL. HD.	NO. 8 – 1 1/4 LONG	4
6	NAIL – FINISH	6 d	16

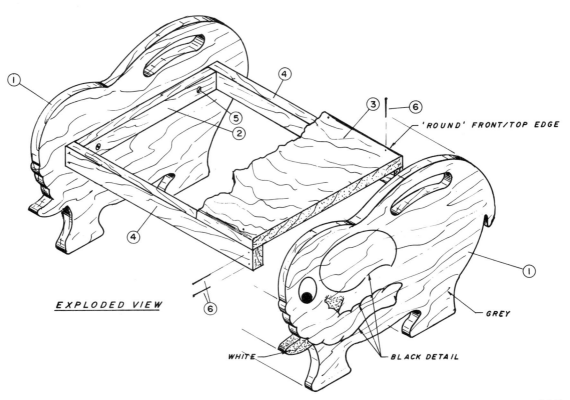

①

⑤
②

④

③

⑥

'ROUND' FRONT/TOP EDGE

④

①

GREY

⑥

EXPLODED VIEW

WHITE

BLACK DETAIL

41♦Noah's Ark with Animals

Noah's Ark seems very popular today. I find them at all the big craft fairs I go to; so here is my version. I tried to make it with a "folk art" flair.

Instructions

♦1 Study the exploded view before starting. Note that the boat sides, parts number 4, are simply nailed or glued to a frame made up of parts number 1, 2, and 3.

♦2 Cut all pieces to overall size according to the cutting list.

♦3 Make up the frame subassembly as shown, using parts number 1, 2, and 3.

♦4 Lay out the two side pieces, parts number 4, using the given dimensions. Drill the three 1-inch-diameter holes.

♦5 On *one* side panel, locate the door and make the two notches. Drill the 1/16-inch-diameter holes for the nails, parts number 7.

  Note: Drill the two 1/16-inch-diameter holes 2¼ inches deep *before* cutting out the door.

♦6 Cut out the door. (Continued on the following three pages.)

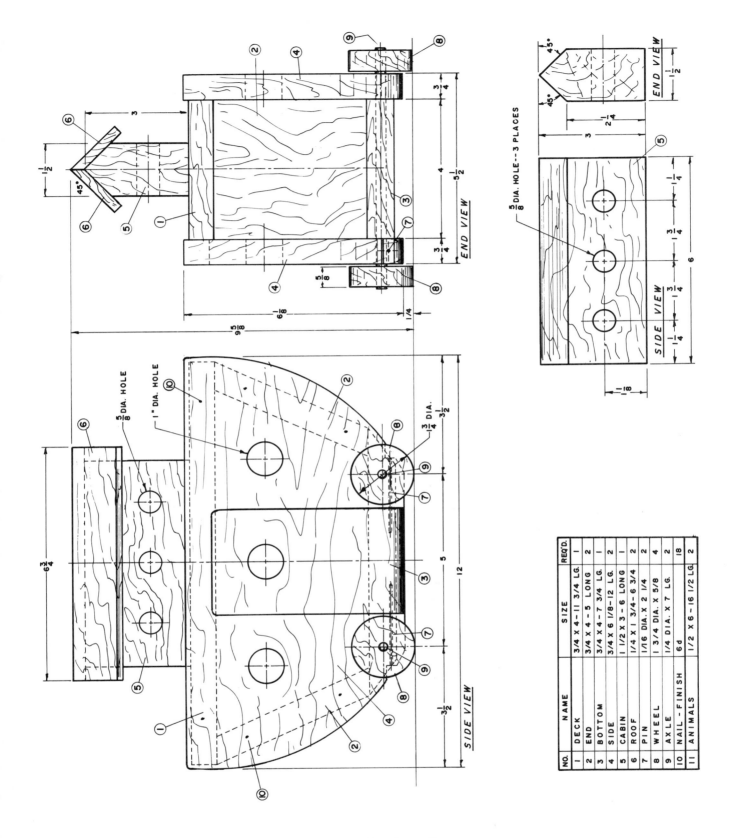

NO.	NAME	SIZE	REQ'D.
I	DECK	3/4 X 4 – 11 3/4 LG.	I
2	END	3/4 X 4 – 5 LONG	2
3	BOTTOM	3/4 X 4 – 7 3/4 LG.	I
4	SIDE	3/4 X 6 1/8 – 12 LG.	2
5	CABIN	I 1/2 X 3 – 6 LONG	I
6	ROOF	I/4 X I 3/4 – 6 3/4	2
7	PIN	I/16 DIA. X 2 I/4	2
8	WHEEL	I 3/4 DIA. X 5/8	4
9	AXLE	I/4 DIA. X 7 LG.	2
10	NAIL – FINISH	6d	18
11	ANIMALS	I/2 X 6 – 16 I/2 LG.	2

♦7 Locate and drill the ¼-inch-diameter holes for the axles, parts number 9.

♦8 Attach the sides, parts number 4, to the frame assembly.

♦9 Sand all over.

117

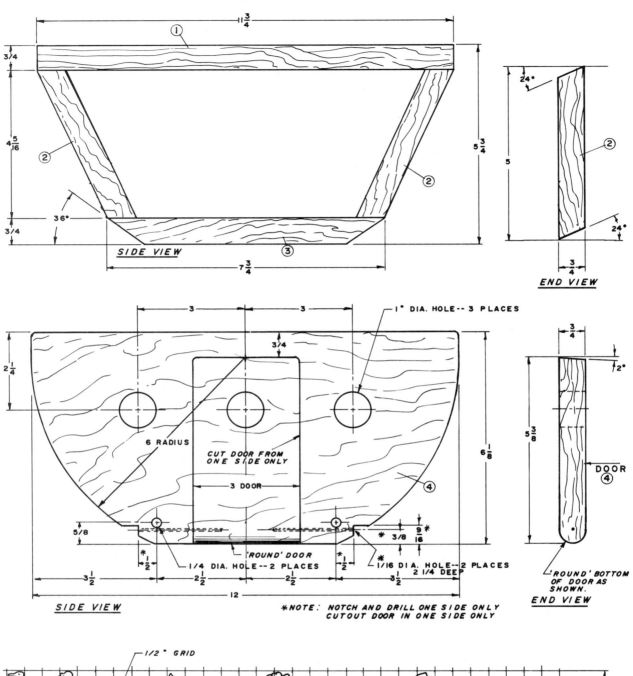

11¾ ①

3/4

4⁵⁄₁₆ ②

②

36°

3/4

SIDE VIEW

7¾

③

5¾

24°

②

5

24°

3/4

END VIEW

3

3

1" DIA. HOLE -- 3 PLACES

3/4

2¼

6 RADIUS

CUT DOOR FROM
ONE SIDE ONLY

3 DOOR

6⅛

④

5/8

9⁄₁₆

* 3/8

*½

*½

'ROUND' DOOR

1/4 DIA. HOLE -- 2 PLACES

1/16 DIA. HOLE -- 2 PLACES
2 1/4 DEEP

3½

2½

2½

3½

12

SIDE VIEW

*NOTE: NOTCH AND DRILL ONE SIDE ONLY
CUTOUT DOOR IN ONE SIDE ONLY

3/4

2°

5³⁄₈

DOOR
④

'ROUND' BOTTOM
OF DOOR AS
SHOWN.

END VIEW

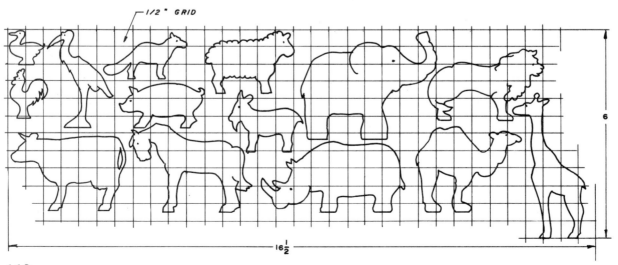

1/2" GRID

6

16½

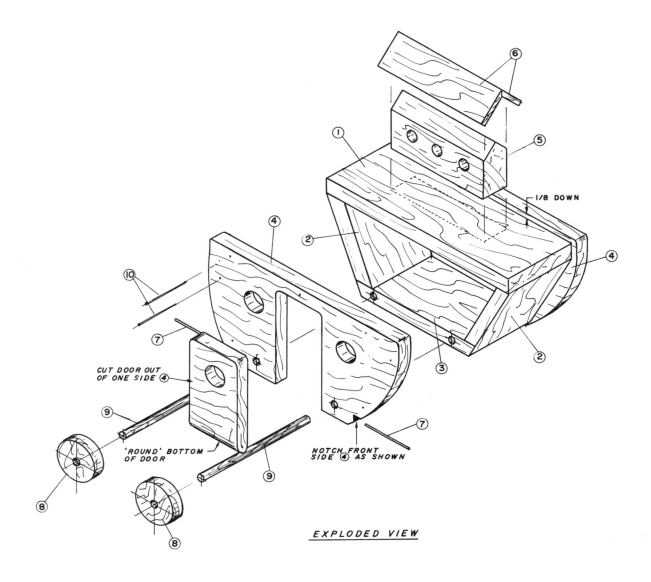

1/8 DOWN

CUT DOOR OUT
OF ONE SIDE ④

'ROUND' BOTTOM
OF DOOR

NOTCH FRONT
SIDE ④ AS SHOWN

EXPLODED VIEW

♦10 Redrill the ¼-inch-diameter holes for the axles through the bottom, part number 3. (You might want to drill a ⁵⁄₁₆-inch-diameter hole so the axle will turn more easily.)

♦11 Make up the remaining pieces, 5 and 6.

♦12 Install the door using the 2 pins, parts number 7.

♦13 Add the axles and wheels (glue the wheels to the axle). Check that they turn freely.

♦14 Paint to suit.

♦15 On a ½-inch grid, lay out the animals, parts number 11. (Use ½-inch-thick wood.) Make *two* of each animal. You might wish to make one set slightly smaller to represent the female of each. (But remember that for some animals, lions for instance, the male and female look quite different.)

♦16 Paint the animals to suit. If you use a nice hardwood they *could* be left natural. You are all set for the next "flood."

42 ◆ Mexican Child's Chair, circa 1930

This project was copied directly from a Mexican child's chair that is at least 50 years old. One of my neighbors, Fred Miller, collects and restores these wonderful old chairs for his nieces and nephews. Of all the Mexican child's chairs he has restored he tells me this one is his favorite. The original was brightly painted and had the floral pattern exactly as illustrated. You will need a lathe to do this project. There are companies that do custom turnings, if you do *not* have a lathe.

You will also have to cane the chair. I, personally, do *not* cane; so if you don't either, have the chair caned for you. Ask for a "diamond pattern" using ¼-inch ash splint.

Instructions

◆1 Cut all pieces to overall size according to the cutting list. Add an inch or two to the legs for turning.

◆2 Turn the legs, parts number 1 and 2, as shown. Sand smooth.

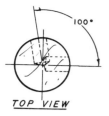

TOP VIEW

NO.	NAME	SIZE	REQ'D.
1	BACK LEG	1 5/8 DIA. -17 LONG	2
2	FRONT LEG	1 5/8 DIA. - 8 1/2 LG.	2
3	STRETCHER	3/4 DIA. -11 3/4 LG.	2
4	STRETCHER	3/4 DIA. - 8 7/8 LG.	6
5	BACK - TOP	1" X 2 - 8 3/4 LONG	1
6	BACK - BOTTOM	1" X 1 1/4 - 8 3/4	1

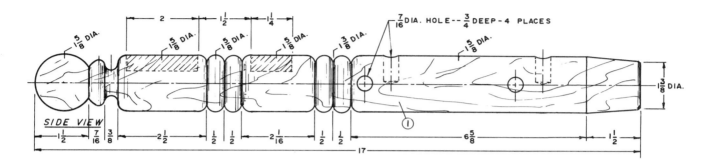

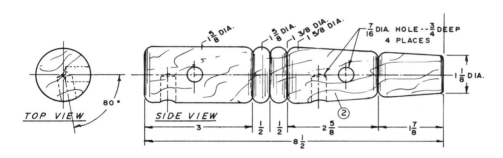

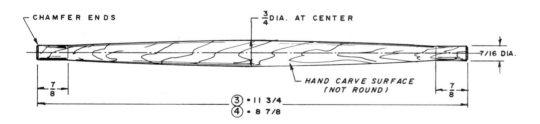

♦3 The stretchers, parts number 3 and 4, are very rough; in fact, the originals were actually *carved* with a spoke knife and *not* truly round. To add character, use a spoke knife.

♦4 Carefully, locate the 7/16-inch-diameter holes in the legs, parts number 1 and 2. Refer to the *top view* of the legs. Note that the holes are drilled at angles to each other of 80 degrees and 100 degrees, as shown. Be sure to make *right-hand* and *left-hand* pairs of the legs.

♦5 Locate and make the two mortises in the back legs, parts number 1, according to the given dimensions. (Make a matching *pair*.)

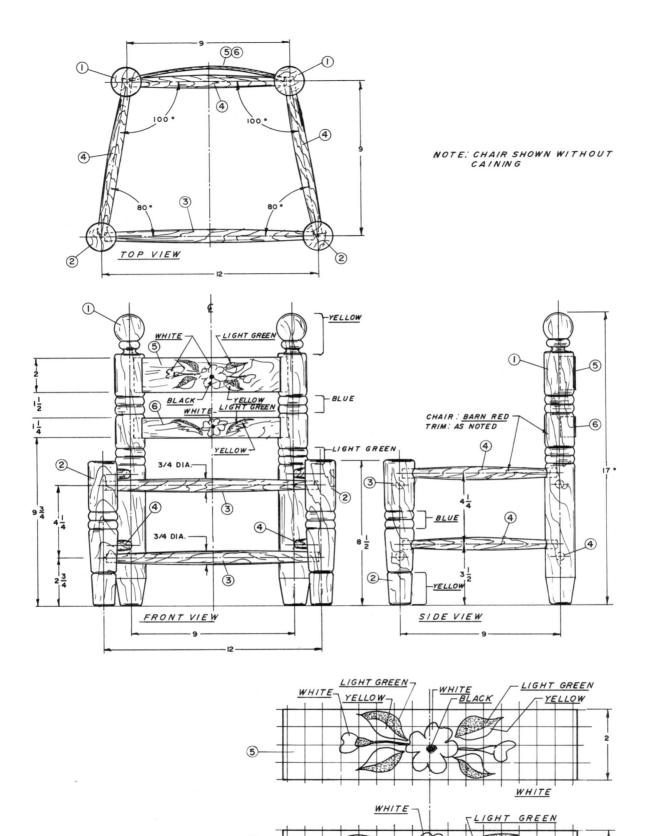

NOTE: CHAIR SHOWN WITHOUT CAINING

9

⑤⑥

①   ①

④   ④

100°   100°

9

④   ④

80°   ③   80°

②   ②

TOP VIEW

12

YELLOW

WHITE   LIGHT GREEN

⑤

BLUE

BLACK   YELLOW
WHITE   LIGHT GREEN

⑥

YELLOW

LIGHT GREEN

CHAIR: BARN RED
TRIM: AS NOTED

②   ②

3/4 DIA.

③

④   ④

③

BLUE

3/4 DIA.

③   ④

9¾   4¼

8½

③   YELLOW

2¾

③

FRONT VIEW

9

12

①   ⑤

⑥

④

③

17°

④   ④

4¼

4¼

3½

②

SIDE VIEW

9

LIGHT GREEN

WHITE   WHITE   LIGHT GREEN
YELLOW   BLACK   YELLOW

⑤

2

WHITE

WHITE   LIGHT GREEN

⑥

1¼

BLACK   YELLOW

½" GRID

PAINTING DETAIL

122

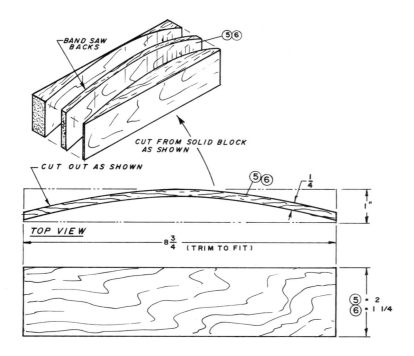

BAND SAW
BACKS

⑤⑥

CUT FROM SOLID BLOCK
AS SHOWN

CUT OUT AS SHOWN

⑤⑥

$\frac{1}{4}$

1"

TOP VIEW

$8\frac{3}{4}$ (TRIM TO FIT)

⑤ = 2
⑥ = 1 1/4

FRONT VIEW

◆6   Using wood 1 inch thick, cut the two backs, parts number 5 and 6, according to the given dimensions. Sand all over.

◆7   Dry-fit all pieces—make corrections, as necessary.

◆8   Glue the chair together. On unusual projects like this, I use an elastic cord to hold it all together while I wait for the glue to set up.

◆9   Prime all over, and lightly sand.

◆10   Paint to suit. The original colors are noted.

◆11   If you want to copy the original floral designs, lay them out on a ½-inch grid. You might consider stencilling them on the chair back.

◆12   Either cane the chair yourself or have it caned for you. Use a ¼-inch-wide flat ash splint material. My neighbor, Fred, weaves a beautiful diamond pattern into his caning which really adds a lot to the chair's look.
   You now have an "authentic" Mexican child's chair.

TOYS FROM YESTERDAY

43 ♦ Cargo Ship, circa 1942

This is a great project to make with scrap materials. It is made from material 1⅛ inch thick by 1¾ inch wide and 5¼ inch long. As a child in the early 1940s, I can remember these little boats were very popular. This is an exact copy of one of those original 1942 toys.

Instructions

♦1   Cut the wood to overall size. (See Step 1.)

♦2   Make the *profile* cut, as shown. (See Step 2.)

♦3   Locate and drill the two ⅞-inch-diameter holes and the one ⅜-inch-diameter hole, as shown.

♦4   Make the final hull cut. Set the saw at an angle from vertical of about 8 degrees.

♦5   Trim the top half of the ship at about 15 degrees, as shown. Use a rasp or a sander.

♦6   Add the smoke stack, part number 2. (Glue in place.)

♦7   The "*cargo*," parts number 3, is simply a ¾-inch-diameter dowel cut ¾ inch long.

♦8   Sand all over.

♦9   Paint to suit. The original was painted as shown.

♦10   Your children and grandchildren will experience the same things that children 50 years ago did when they play with this toy boat.

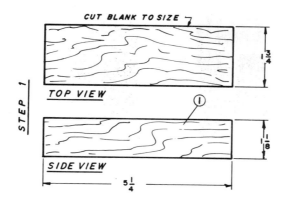

CUT BLANK TO SIZE

TOP VIEW

1 1/4

SIDE VIEW

① 1 1/8

5 1/4

STEP 1

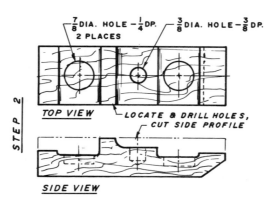

7/8 DIA. HOLE — 1/4 DP.
2 PLACES

3/8 DIA. HOLE — 3/8 DP.

TOP VIEW

LOCATE & DRILL HOLES,
CUT SIDE PROFILE

SIDE VIEW

STEP 2

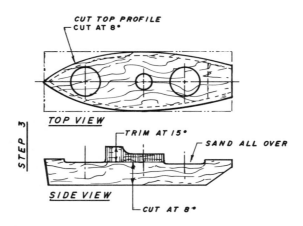

CUT TOP PROFILE
CUT AT 8°

TOP VIEW

TRIM AT 15°

SAND ALL OVER

SIDE VIEW

CUT AT 8°

STEP 3

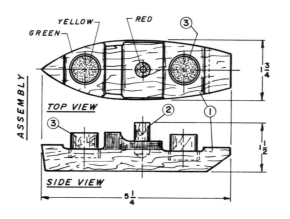

YELLOW

RED

GREEN

③

TOP VIEW

1 1/4

③

②

①

1 1/2

SIDE VIEW

5 1/4

ASSEMBLY

125

44 ◆ Bobbing-Head Bank, circa 1930

I found this toy at a local antique shop. After purchasing it I have seen many versions of this exact same toy. I found it very interesting; so I thought you might, too. You will need a lathe to make this project.

Instructions

◆ 1   Cut all parts to overall size.

◆ 2   Turn the body, part number 1, head, part number 2, and nose, part number 3, using given dimensions.

◆ 3   Carefully drill out the interior of the body at a 1½ inch diameter, 5⅝ inches deep. Add the 2-inch-diameter step, as shown.

◆ 4   Sand all over. (Continued on the following two pages.)

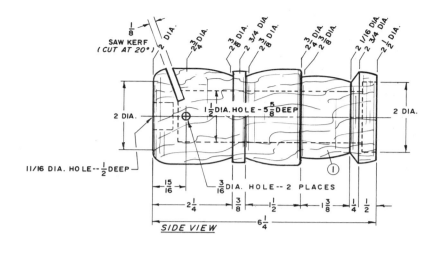

SIDE VIEW

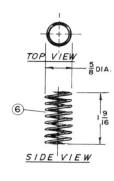

FRONT VIEW

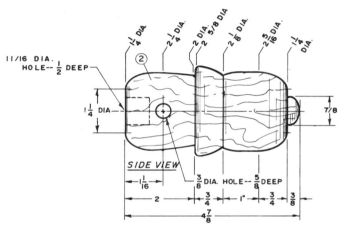

SIDE VIEW

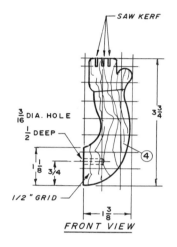

NO.	NAME	SIZE	REQ'D.
1	BODY	2 3/4 DIA. – 6 1/4 LG.	1
2	HEAD	2 5/8 DIA. – 4 7/8 LG.	1
3	NOSE	5/8 DIA. – 1 1/2 LONG	1
4	ARM	1/2 X 1 3/8 – 3 3/4	2
5	PEG	3/16 DIA. – 1 1/8 LONG	2
6	SPRING	5/8 DIA. – 1 9/16 LG.	1
7	CAP	2 DIA. X 1/4 THICK	1
8	SCREW–RD. HD.	NO. 4 – 5/8 LONG	2

♦5 Locate and drill all holes in the body and head, using given dimensions.

♦6 Carefully locate and make the ⅛-inch-thick saw kerf at an angle of 20 degrees, as shown. This is the slot.

♦7 On a ½-inch grid, lay out the arms, parts number 4.

♦8 Transfer to the wood and cut out. Sand all over.

♦9 Glue the spring to the head and body, preferably with epoxy. (The spring can be purchased from most hardware stores.)

♦10 Glue the arms to the body, as shown—one *up* and one *down*.

♦11 Glue the nose, part number 3, in place.

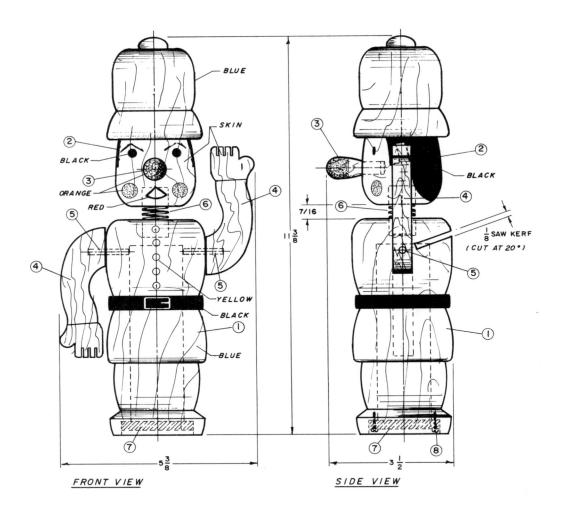

FRONT VIEW   SIDE VIEW

♦12   Make a 2-inch-diameter cap, part number 7, and fasten it to the body with screws, parts number 8.

♦13   Prime and lightly sand.

♦14   Paint to suit. Suggested colors are noted, if you want yours like the original.

45 ◆ Eating Chickens, circa 1880

This toy really goes back in time; it is over 100 years old. I have seen many versions of this, but I found this particular one to be one of the nicest. A local antique dealer, Marny Bean, let me borrow it so that I could include it here. These chickens were very popular with children in the late 1800s. Sometimes simple toys *are* the best!

Note: These chickens require some carving which is different from most of the projects.

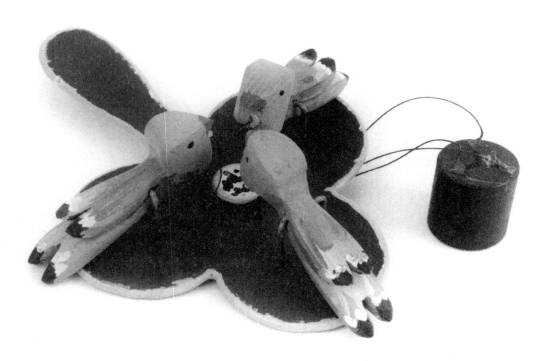

Instructions

◆1   Cut all pieces to overall size.

◆2   Make the base, part number 1, according to the pattern.

◆3   Locate and drill all holes, as shown.

◆4   Make up the dish, part number 4, and glue it in place to the base, part number 1.

◆5   Carve the chickens, parts number 2, approximately as shown. Remember that they don't have to be exact.

◆6   Locate and drill the two ¹⁄₁₆-inch-diameter hole in each, as shown; one for the foot, part number 3, the other for the string, part number 5.

◆7   Make up the weight, part number 6, out of a heavy piece of hardwood. Drill three ¹⁄₁₆-inch-diameter holes in line with the three ³⁄₁₆-inch-diameter holes in the base.

(Continued on the following two pages.)

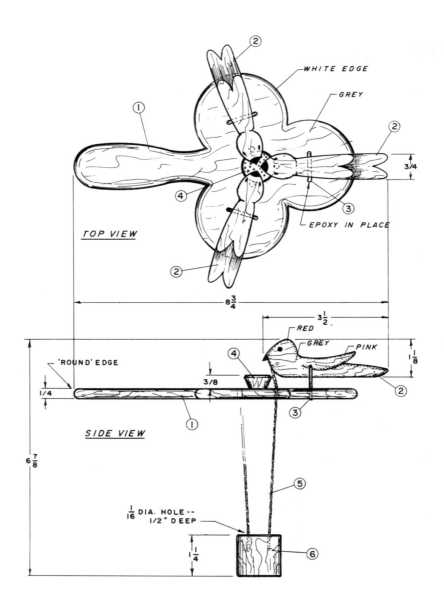

② —— WHITE EDGE

—— GREY

TOP VIEW

3/4

EPOXY IN PLACE

8 3/4

3 1/2

—— RED

GREY   PINK

'ROUND' EDGE

1/4

3/8

SIDE VIEW

1 1/8

6 7/8

1/16 DIA. HOLE --
1/2" DEEP

1 1/4

NO.	NAME	SIZE	REQ'D.
1	BASE	1/4 X 5 1/2 - 8 LG.	1
2	BIRD	3/4 X 1 1/8 - 3 1/2 LG.	3
3	FOOT (WIRE)	1/16 DIA. X 2 7/8 LG.	3
4	DISH	7/8 DIA. X 3/8 LG.	1
5	STRING	6" LONG	3
6	WEIGHT-HARDWOOD	1 1/4 DIA. X 1 1/4	1

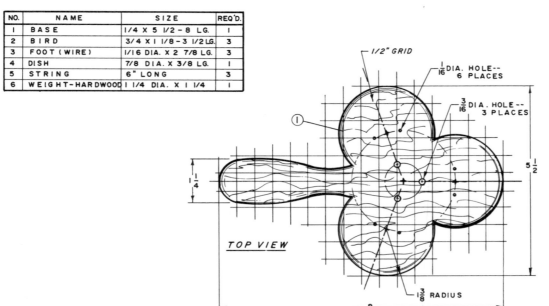

1/2" GRID

1/16 DIA. HOLE --
6 PLACES

3/16 DIA. HOLE --
3 PLACES

5 1/2

1 1/4

TOP VIEW

1 3/8 RADIUS

8

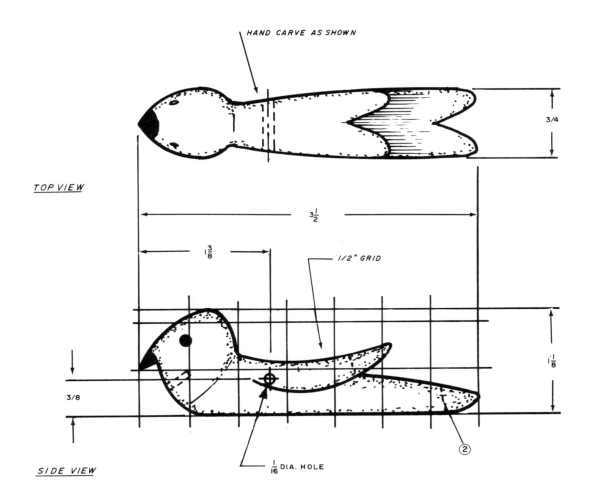

HAND CARVE AS SHOWN

TOP VIEW

3/4

3½

1¾⁄8

1/2" GRID

1⅛

3/8

1/16 DIA. HOLE

②

SIDE VIEW

♦8 Using wire such as a coat hanger, push the wire through each chicken's body and bend down on the sides. Make sure the chickens move freely.

♦9 Glue the wire to the base, part number 1, preferably with epoxy.

♦10 Glue the string, part number 5, into the front of each chicken's body down through the 3/16-inch-diameter holes in the base and into a hole in the weight, part number 6.

♦11 Check that the chickens move freely.

♦12 Paint to suit. The original base was grey with a white edge.

46♦Tractor-Trailer, circa 1948

This is a wonderful truck I found in an antique shop in St. Johnsbury, Vermont. It was probably made right after World War II. I'm not sure if it was commercially made or homemade. It looked a little of both. Either way, it makes a nice, simple project even for today.

Instructions

♦1   Cut parts to overall size according to the cutting list.

♦2   Using the given dimensions, lay out and cut out the cab, part number 1, and the support, part number 6.

♦3   Sand all over.

♦4   Glue the donut, part number 7, and headlights, parts number 12, to the cab.

♦5   Glue the side rails, front rail, and rear rail in place. Sand all edges.

♦6   Add the pin, part number 8.

♦7   Glue the support, part number 6, in place.

♦8   Sand all over, rounding all edges slightly.
(Continued on the following two pages.)

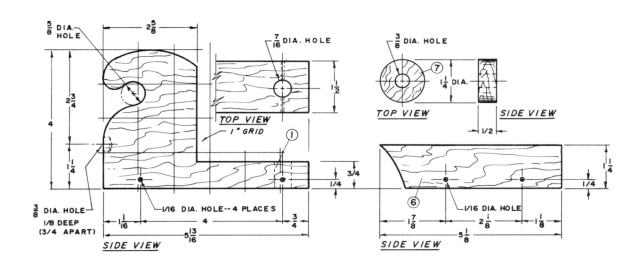

NO.	NAME	SIZE	REQ'D.
1	CAB	1 1/2 X 4 - 5 13/16 LG.	1
2	TRUCK	3/4 X 3 - 11 5/8 LG.	1
3	SIDE RAIL	5/16 X 5/16 - 11 5/8	2
4	FRONT RAIL	5/16 X 3/4 - 2 3/8	1
5	REAR RAIL	5/16 X 5/16 - 2 3/8	1
6	SUPPORT	1 1/4 X 1 1/2 - 5 1/8	1
7	DONUT	1 1/4 DIA. X 1/2 LG.	1
8	PIN	3/8 DIA. X 1 3/4	1
9	WHEEL	1 3/4 DIA. X 5/8 LG.	8
10	SCREW—RD. HD.	NO. 6 X 1 3/4 LG.	8
11	WASHER	SMALL	16
12	HEADLIGHT	3/8 DIA. X 1/4 LG.	2

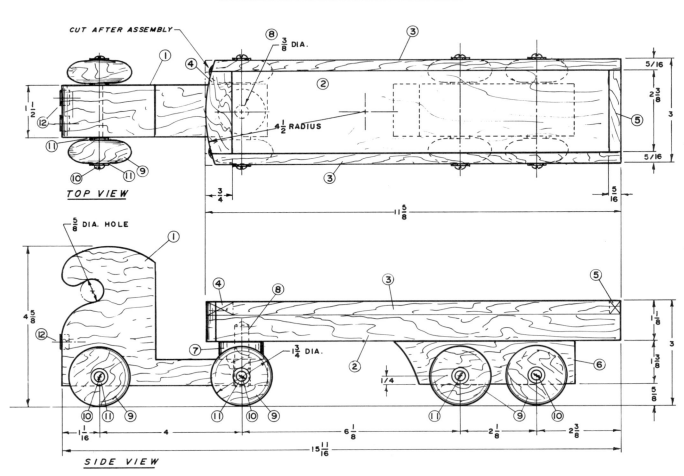

133

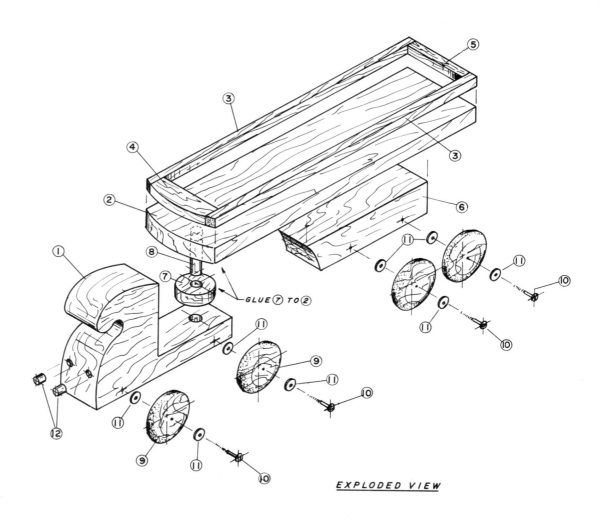

EXPLODED VIEW

♦9   Prime and paint to suit.

♦10   Add wheels, parts number 9, with washers and screws, as shown.

47♦Book House, circa 1925

This unusual, original bookcase was found in Surry, New Hampshire. It was sold by Christian Scientists back in the 1920s. A set of children's books filled the house. Books, I feel, are an important toy for children of all ages. This makes a neat place to store your child's books. I would suggest you make it out of high-grade plywood.

Instructions

♦1　Cut all pieces to overall size according to the cutting list. Use high-grade plywood for the ends, parts number 1, back, part number 3, and roof, parts number 4 and 5.

♦2　Using the detailed plan, lay out the ends, parts number 1; cut out and sand all edges. (*Temporarily* tack the two sides together *before* cutting and sanding.) (Continued on the following three pages.)

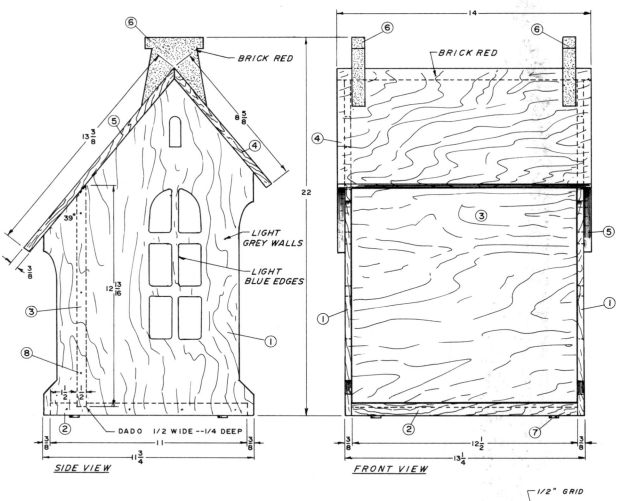

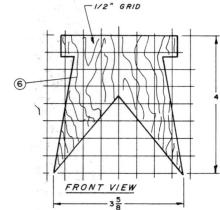

BRICK RED

LIGHT GREY WALLS

LIGHT BLUE EDGES

13 3/8

8 5/8

39°

3/8

12 13/16

DADO 1/2 WIDE --1/4 DEEP

11

11 3/4

SIDE VIEW

14

BRICK RED

22

12 1/2

13 1/4

FRONT VIEW

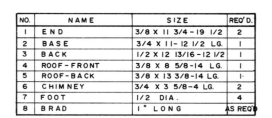

1/2" GRID

FRONT VIEW

3 5/8

4

NO.	NAME	SIZE	REQ'D.
1	END	3/8 X 11 3/4 - 19 1/2	2
2	BASE	3/4 X 11 - 12 1/2 LG.	1
3	BACK	1/2 X 12 13/16 - 12 1/2	1
4	ROOF-FRONT	3/8 X 8 5/8 - 14 LG.	1
5	ROOF-BACK	3/8 X 13 3/8 - 14 LG.	1
6	CHIMNEY	3/4 X 3 5/8 - 4 LG.	2
7	FOOT	1/2 DIA.	4
8	BRAD	1" LONG	AS REQ'D

◆ 3   Make the ½-inch-wide by ¼-inch-deep dado in the base, part number 2, 1½ inches back from back edge, as shown.

◆ 4   Cut the top edge of the back, part number 3, at an angle of 39 degrees, as shown.

◆ 5   Cut the top edges of the roof pieces, parts number 4 and 5, at an angle as close to 39 degrees as you can manage.

◆ 6   Lay out and cut out the chimney, part number 6.

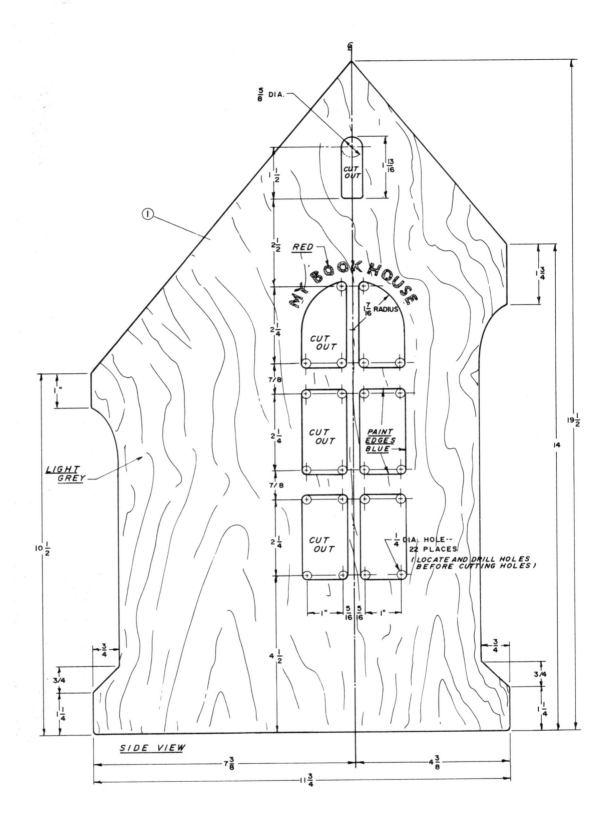

SIDE VIEW

♦ 7 Assemble all pieces with glue and nails. (The exploded view is on the next page.)

♦ 8 Set nails, and fill all nail holes.

♦ 9 Sand all over; "round" all sharp edges.

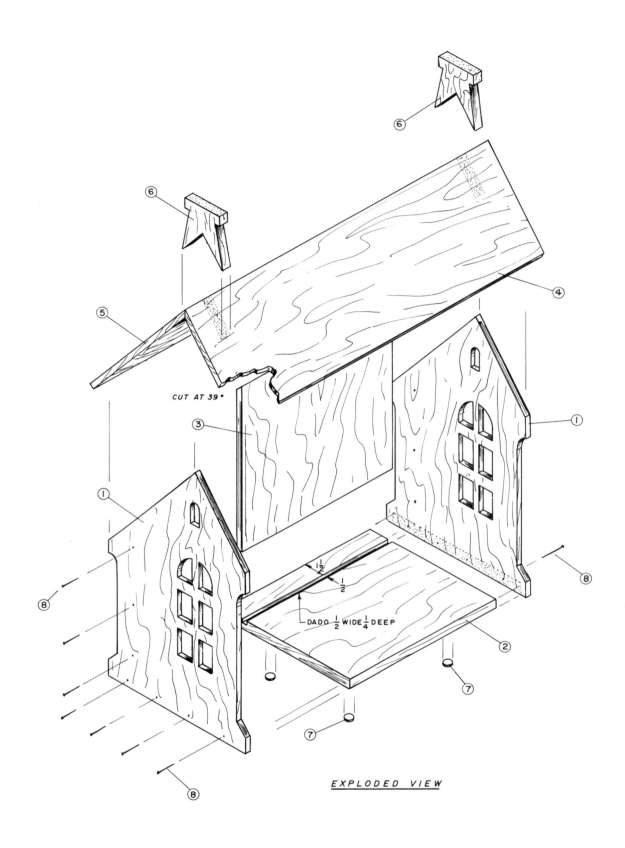

CUT AT 39°

DADO $\frac{1}{2}$ WIDE $\frac{1}{4}$ DEEP

EXPLODED VIEW

◆10   Paint to suit. The original was painted light grey with edges light bone; the roof was brick red. It had *"My Book House"* letters above the window, as shown.

◆11   Add four rubber feet, parts number 7.

48♦Grasshopper, circa 1910

Here is another old pull toy that I found in southern Vermont—or at least, *most* of it. It was in pretty bad condition, but enough was there to record what it must have looked like. The original had a noisemaker. If you don't want it, omit the notch in the body and omit parts number 9, 11, and 12.

Instructions

♦ 1   Before starting, carefully study the exploded view. Be sure you understand how it all goes together.

♦ 2   Cut all pieces to overall size according to the cutting list.

♦ 3   Glue up two ½-inch-thick pieces for the body, part number 1, if you don't have 1-inch-thick material.

♦ 4   Using a 1-inch grid, lay out the body, part number 1. Note all holes and the location of the notch.

♦ 5   Carefully make the ½-inch-wide notch in the body before cutting out the body.

♦ 6   Drill all holes in the body.

♦ 7   Cut out the shape of the body, and sand all over.

♦ 8   Using a ½-inch grid, lay out the legs, parts number 2, 15, and 17.

♦ 9   Cut out two pairs of each leg, and drill following the given dimensions. (Continued on the following two pages.)

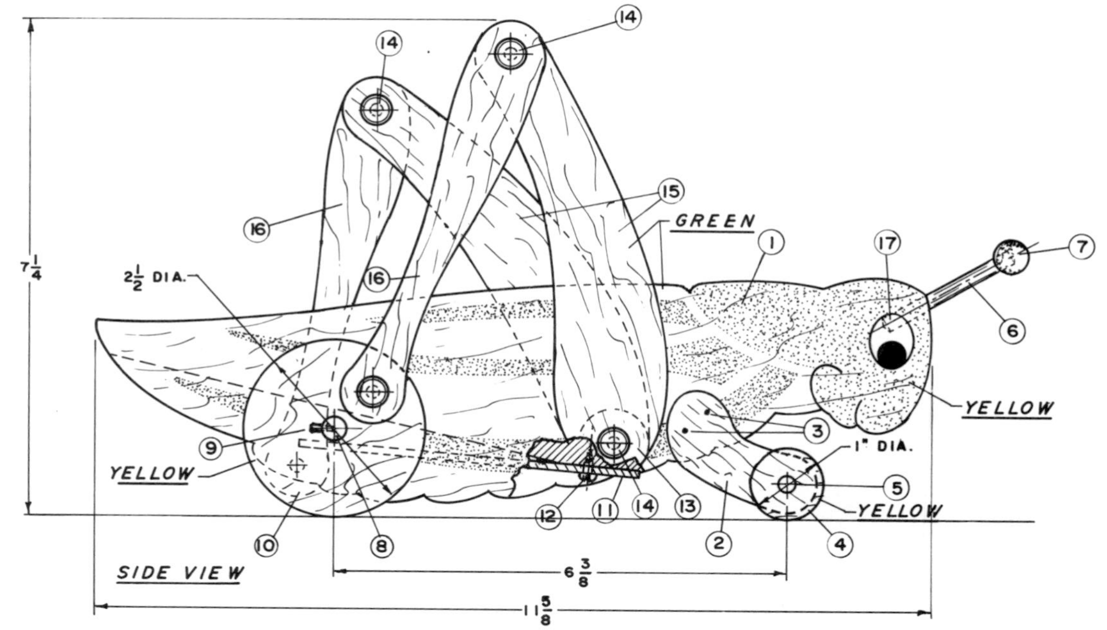
SIDE VIEW
7 1/4
2 1/2 DIA.
GREEN
YELLOW
YELLOW
1" DIA.
YELLOW
6 3/8
11 5/8

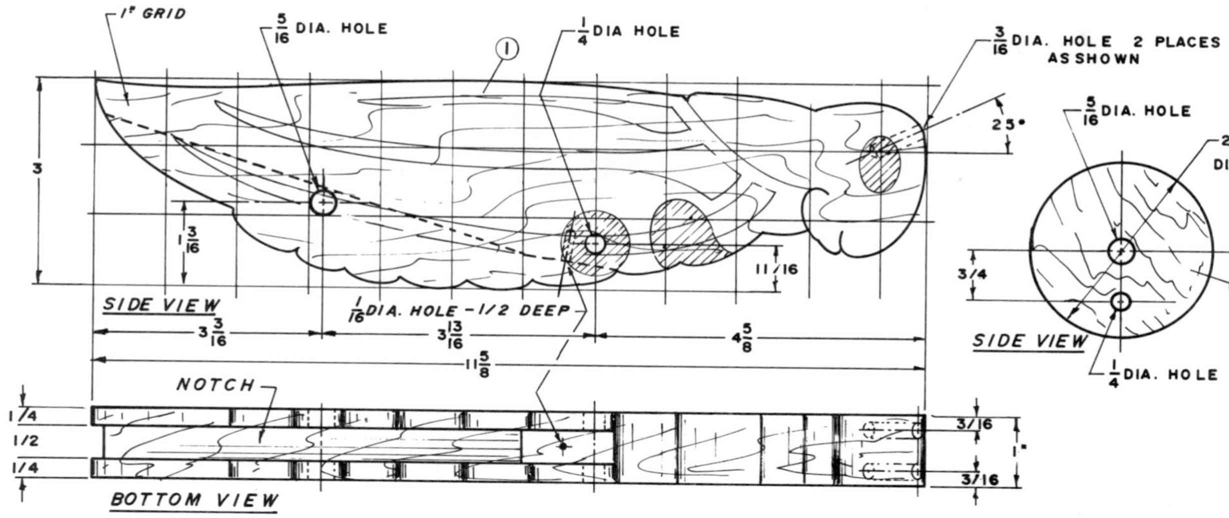
1" GRID
5/16 DIA. HOLE
1/4 DIA HOLE
3/16 DIA. HOLE 2 PLACES AS SHOWN
25°
3
1 3/16
11/16
SIDE VIEW
1/16 DIA. HOLE - 1/2 DEEP
3 3/16
3 13/16
4 5/8
11 5/8
5/16 DIA. HOLE
2 1/2 DIA.
3/4
SIDE VIEW
1/4 DIA. HOLE
NOTCH
1/4
1/2
1/4
3/16
1"
3/16
BOTTOM VIEW

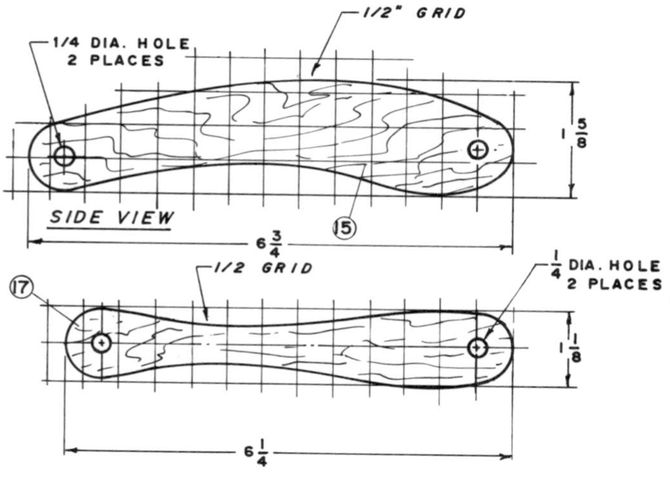
1/4 DIA. HOLE 2 PLACES
1/2" GRID
1 5/8
SIDE VIEW
6 3/4
1/2 GRID
1/4 DIA. HOLE 2 PLACES
1 1/8
6 1/4

NO.	NAME	SIZE	REQ'D.
1	BODY	1 X 3 - 11 5/8 LONG	1
2	FRONT LEG	1/4 X 1 1/4 - 2 1/2	2
3	BRAD	1" LONG	4
4	WHEEL	1" DIA. - 3/8 LONG	2
5	AXLE	1/4 DIA. - 1 5/8 LG.	1
6	ANTENNA	3/16 DIA. - 2 LONG	2
7	SPHERE	1/2 SIZE	2
8	AXLE	5/16 DIA. - 1 7/8	1
9	CAM	1/8 X 1/4 - 3/8 LG.	1
10	WHEEL	2 1/2 DIA. - 1/2 LG.	2
11	CLICKER	1/16 X 3/8 - 4 3/4	1
12	SCREW - RD. HD.	NO. 6 - 3/4 LONG	1
13	SPACER	1" DIA. - 3/32 LONG	2
14	PEG	1/4 DIA.	6
15	BACK LEG	7/16 X 1 5/8 - 6 3/4	2
16	BACK LEG	3/8 X 1 1/8 - 6 1/4	2
17	JIGGLE EYE	3/4 OVAL	2

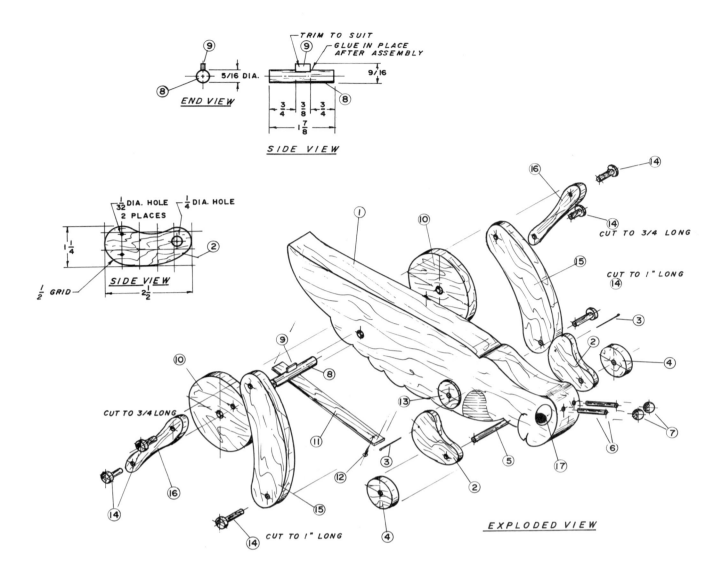

TRIM TO SUIT

9

GLUE IN PLACE
AFTER ASSEMBLY

5/16 DIA.

8

END VIEW

9/16

3/4 3/8 3/4

1 7/8

SIDE VIEW

1/32 DIA. HOLE
2 PLACES

1/4 DIA. HOLE

1 1/4

SIDE VIEW

1/2 GRID

2 1/2

CUT TO 3/4 LONG

CUT TO 1" LONG

CUT TO 3/4 LONG

CUT TO 1" LONG

EXPLODED VIEW

♦10   Add the two antennas, parts number 6, and spheres, parts number 7, to body.

♦11   Glue the spacers, parts number 13, to the body.

♦12   Glue and nail the front legs, parts number 2, in place.

♦13   Make up the wheels, parts number 10, as shown.

♦14   Assemble according to the exploded view. Check that the legs move freely.

♦15   Add the clicker, part number 11 (optional), and check that it clicks correctly.

♦16   Paint to suit. (Refer to the side view of the body for painting details.)

49 ◆ World War I Aeroplane, circa 1916

Here comes the "Red Baron" in his red triplane. Children are usually fascinated with planes; so here is a very old "aeroplane" for them with a lot of history, too. In World War I it was a notorious German airplane—and a favorite among history buffs and children alike ever since. (Planes such as this toy are also fun to *make*.)

Instructions

◆1   Cut all pieces to overall size according to the cutting list. Sand all over.

◆2   Glue up two ¾-inch-thick pieces to make up the body, part number 1.

◆3   Stack all three wings; cut and drill them at the same time. Note that the *top* wing has four extra scallop cutouts in the center and that the middle wing will have to be *cut* to fit the body.

◆4   Cut out the body profile, part number 1. Round the front section, as shown.

◆5   Locate and drill all holes in the body. Sand all over.
(Continued on the following three pages.)

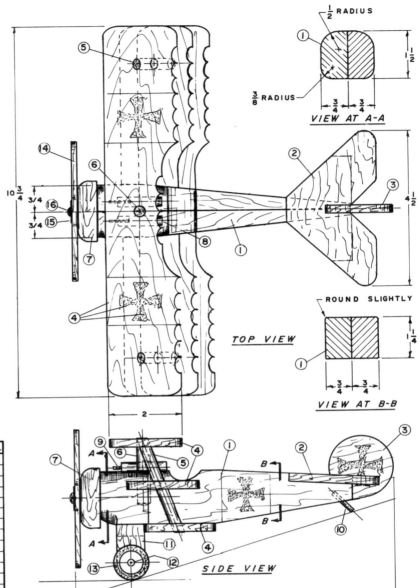

VIEW AT A-A

½ RADIUS

1½

¾ RADIUS

¾   ¾

TOP VIEW

VIEW AT B-B

ROUND SLIGHTLY

1¼

¾   ¾

NO.	NAME	SIZE	REQ'D.
I	BODY	3/4 X 1 5/8 - 7 1/8 LG.	2
2	ELEVATOR	1/4 X 2 1/2 - 4 1/2	1
3	RUDDER	1/4 X 1 7/8 - 1 7/8 LG.	1
4	WING	1/4 X 2 1/8 - 10 3/4	3
5	STRUTT	3/8 DIA. - 3 1/8 LG.	2
6	BRACE	3/8 DIA. - 2 LG.	1
7	COWL	1 3/4 DIA. - 1/2 LG.	1
8	GUN BARREL	1/4 DIA. - 1 1/4 LG.	2
9	GUN BARREL	1/8 DIA. - 1/2 LG.	2
10	PIN	1/8 DIA. - 3/4 LG.	1
11	LANDING GEAR	3/4 X 1 1/2 - 2 1/2	1
12	AXLE	3/16 DIA - 3 1/8 LG.	1
13	WHEEL	1" DIA. - 1/4 LONG	4
14	PROP	1/8 X 7/8 - 4 LONG	1
15	WASHER	1/8 SIZE	1
16	SCREW-RD. HD.	NO. 6 - 1" LONG	1

SIDE VIEW

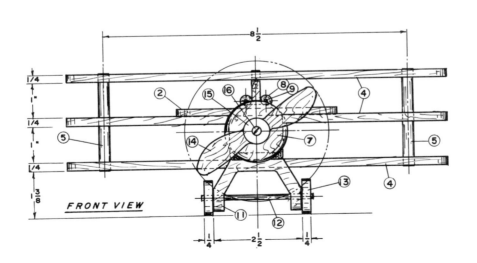

FRONT VIEW

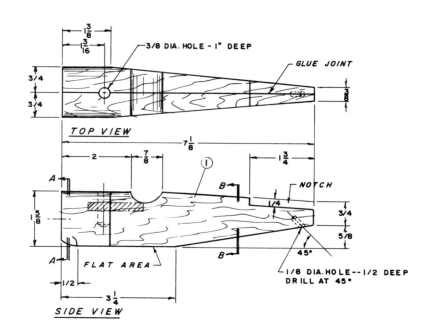

TOP VIEW

3/8 DIA. HOLE - 1" DEEP

GLUE JOINT

3/4

3/4

SIDE VIEW

7 1/8

2

7/8

①

1 3/4

NOTCH

1/4

3/4

5/8

45°

1/8 DIA. HOLE--1/2 DEEP
DRILL AT 45°

A

A

1 5/8

FLAT AREA

B

B

1/2

3 1/4

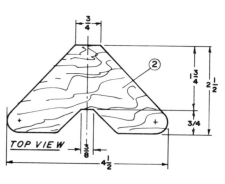

TOP VIEW

3/4

2

1 3/4

2 1/2

3/4

3/8

4 1/2

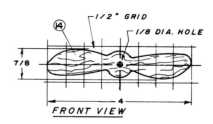

1/2" GRID

1/8 DIA. HOLE

14

7/8

4

FRONT VIEW

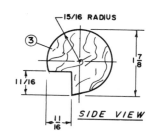

15/16 RADIUS

3

1 7/8

11/16

11/16

SIDE VIEW

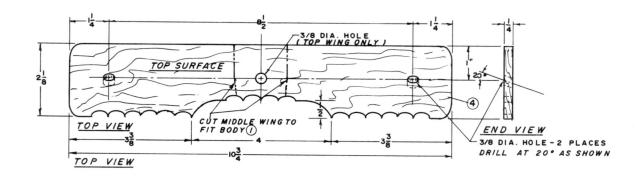

1/4

8 1/2

3/8 DIA. HOLE
(TOP WING ONLY)

1 1/4

1/4

TOP SURFACE

2 1/8

1"

20°

END VIEW

TOP VIEW

CUT MIDDLE WING TO
FIT BODY ①

④

3/8 DIA. HOLE - 2 PLACES
DRILL AT 20° AS SHOWN

3/8

4

3/8

10 3/4

TOP VIEW

1/2

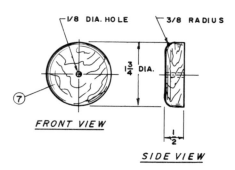

1/8 DIA. HOLE

3/8 RADIUS

1 3/4 DIA.

7

FRONT VIEW

1/2

SIDE VIEW

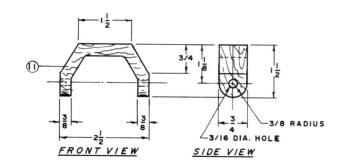

1 1/2

3/4

1 1/8

1 1/2

11

3/8

3/8

2 1/2

FRONT VIEW

3/4

3/8 RADIUS

3/16 DIA. HOLE

SIDE VIEW

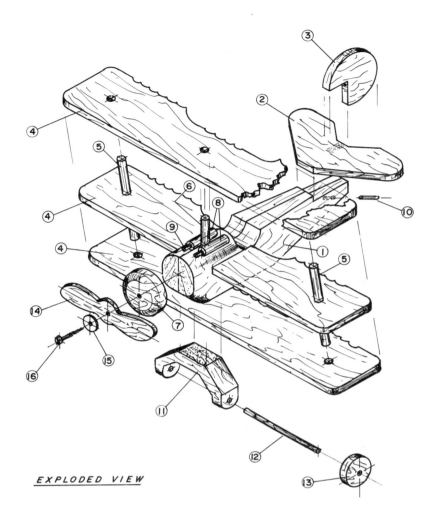

EXPLODED VIEW

♦6   Lay out and cut out the elevator, rudder, cowl, propeller, and landing gear, parts number 2, 3, 7, 14, and 11.

♦7   Make up material for the gun barrel, parts number 8 and 9.

♦8   Round the front edge of the cowl, part number 7.

♦9   Dry-fit all pieces; trim as necessary.

♦10   Glue all pieces together.

♦11   Paint to suit. Red is a good choice for this particular plane. "Snoopy had better watch out; here comes the Red Baron!"

50◆Doll Cradle, circa 1900

Cradles are always a big hit with that "little lady" of the house. This one is just right for a small doll or teddy bear.

Instructions

◆1 Cut all pieces to overall size.

◆2 On a 1-inch grid, lay out the pieces to get a pattern of each.

◆3 Transfer the patterns to the wood and cut out. (Make an *exact* pair of the rockers, parts number 5, and sides, parts number 1.)

◆4 Cut the bottom edge of the sides, parts number 1, at an angle of 16 degrees. Cut the bottom edge of the head and foot, parts number 2 and 3, at an angle of 6 degrees.

◆5 Round the edges of the bottom, part number 4.

◆6 Glue and nail the rockers, parts number 5, to the bottom, part number 4, as shown.

◆7 Glue the top section, parts number 1, 2, and 3, together and nail also with parts number 7.
(Continued on the following two pages.)

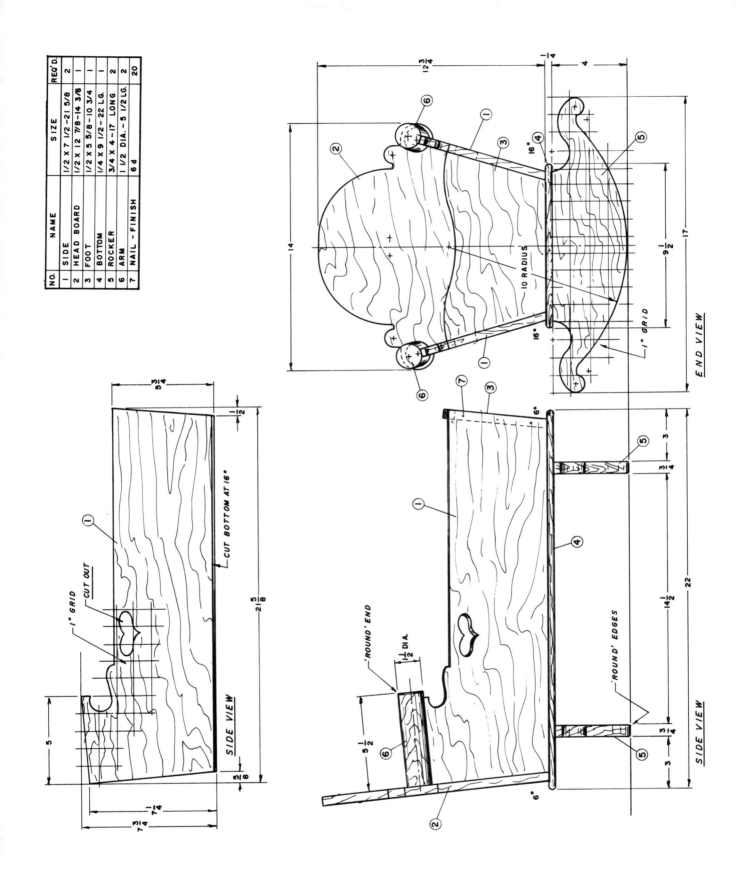

NO.	NAME	SIZE	REQ'D.
1	SIDE	1/2 x 7 1/2 - 21 5/8	2
2	HEAD BOARD	1/2 x 12 7/8 - 14 3/8	1
3	FOOT	1/2 x 5 5/8 - 10 3/4	1
4	BOTTOM	1/4 x 9 1/2 - 22 LG.	1
5	ROCKER	3/4 x 4 - 17 LONG	2
6	ARM	1 1/2 DIA. - 5 1/2 LG.	2
7	NAIL – FINISH	6 d	20

◆8 Sand the top section flat so that it will sit flat on the bottom board, part number 4.

147

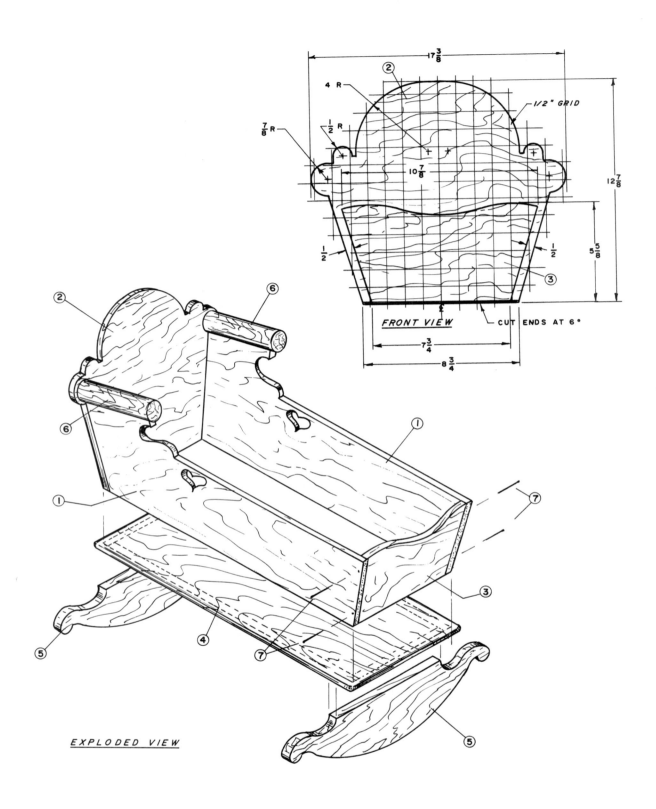

FRONT VIEW

CUT ENDS AT 6°

EXPLODED VIEW

♦ 9 Glue the top section to the bottom board.

♦ 10 Sand all over, and slightly "round" all corners.

♦ 11 Stain or paint to suit. The original was stained, but I found it to be a little dull. I suggest painting the cradle so that it will be bright.

51 ◆ Rocking Horse, circa 1935

What would a toy book be without a rocking horse? I have made a rocking horse for each of my grandchildren, and I think it is by far the most popular toy I have made them—at least until they outgrow it. It has always fascinated me how they seem instinctively to know exactly how to ride the horse. This one is a copy of one I bought at a flea market in southern New Hampshire. It was painted yellow with red and black edges.

Note: This is a very simple project *except* fitting the legs to the seat. Refer to *"view at A-A."* This is a cross section of the final assembly. Note that the ½-inch-diameter holes must be drilled at an angle of 70 degrees, as shown. Fit the *top* section of the legs, parts number 2, to the seat, part number 1.

Instructions

◆1   Cut all pieces to overall size according to the cutting list.

◆2   Lay out the seat, part number 1, following the given dimensions.

◆3   Cut out the seat, and drill all holes. **Important:** Note that the four ¼-inch-diameter holes are drilled *from the bottom* ⅝ inch deep; sand all over.

◆4   On a ½-inch grid, lay out the head, part number 7. Transfer the pattern to the wood and cut out. Sand all over.

◆5   Cut out the tail, part number 9, following the given dimensions. Sand all over. (Continued on the following four pages.)

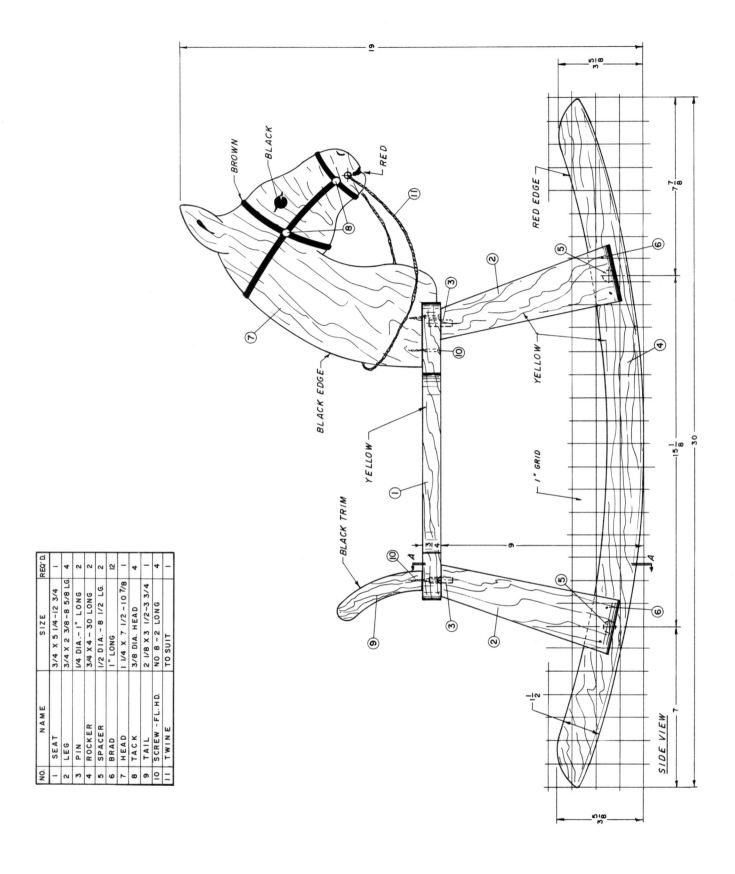

NO.	NAME	SIZE	REQ'D.
1	SEAT	3/4 X 5 1/4 – 12 3/4	1
2	LEG	3/4 X 2 3/8 – 8 5/8 LG.	4
3	PIN	1/4 DIA.– 1" LONG	2
4	ROCKER	3/4 X 4 – 30 LONG	2
5	SPACER	1/2 DIA. – 8 1/2 LG.	2
6	BRAD	1" LONG	12
7	HEAD	1 1/4 X 7 1/2 – 10 7/8	1
8	TACK	3/8 DIA. HEAD	4
9	TAIL	2 1/8 X 3 1/2 – 3 3/4	1
10	SCREW – FL. HD.	NO 8 – 2 LONG	4
11	TWINE	TO SUIT	1

◆6 On a 1-inch grid, lay out the rockers, parts number 4. Transfer the pattern to one of the two rocker pieces.

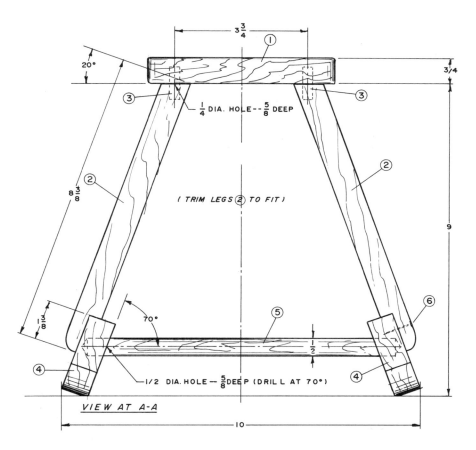

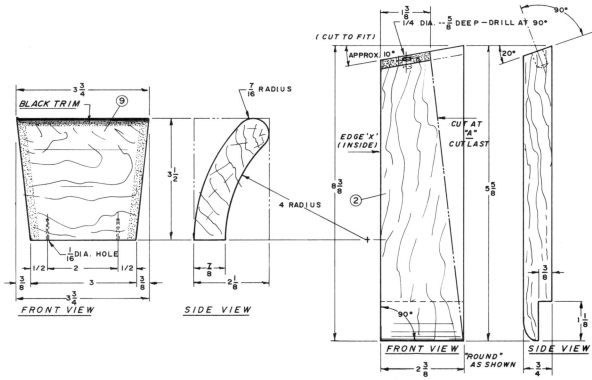

♦7 Tack the two pieces together, and cut out. Sand all over. Be sure to
"round" the bottom edge.

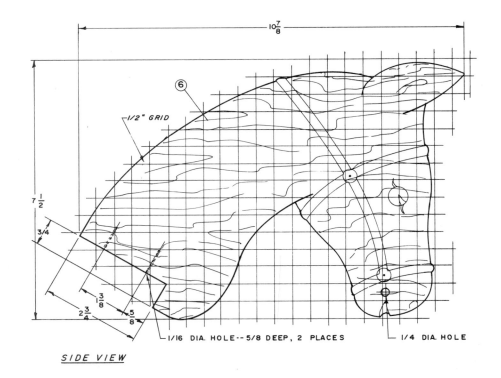

SIDE VIEW

BOTTOM VIEW

♦8 Carefully, cut out the four legs, parts number 2, as shown. (See the front and side views for details.)

♦9 Locate and drill all holes, as shown. In the legs, parts number 2, add dowel pins, parts number 3.

♦10 Dry-fit the legs, parts number 2, and spacers, parts number 5, to the rockers, parts number 4. Use the ¼-inch-diameter holes in the *bottom* of the seat and the pins, parts number 3, as a guide in dry-fitting the pieces. If necessary, trim to suit.

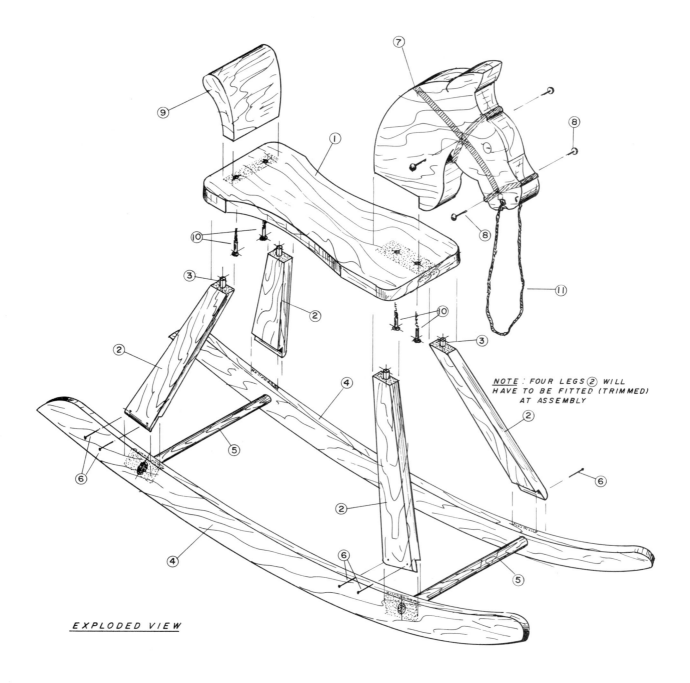

EXPLODED VIEW

NOTE: FOUR LEGS ② WILL
HAVE TO BE FITTED (TRIMMED)
AT ASSEMBLY

♦11   Glue and screw the head and tail to the seat.

♦12   Glue and nail the legs to the rockers and seat. Add the spacers, parts
number 5, at the same time.

♦13   Sand all over, "rounding" all sharp edges.

♦14   Paint to suit. Note the colors that were used on the original horse.
Your horse is ready for the next roundup.

52♦Walking Seesaw, circa 1938

In an old woodworking magazine dated 1938, I saw a project called *Walking Seesaw*. The idea fascinated me so I studied it at length. The base was designed around a parabolic curve, which, when rocked, actually "walks" along. My design is refined from that original idea. Be sure to make it out of a hardwood. Oak or ash really look good and would be my first choice. Use an outdoor, waterproof clear top coat.

Note: The rocker assembly is made from a ¾-inch by 10-inch, 8-foot-long piece of wood.

Instructions

♦1   On a large piece of paper or cardboard (24 inches by 36 inches) lay out the *left* side of the rocker.

♦2   To draw the parabolic curve, divide the *left* vertical side into nine equal, 2-inch spaces (18 inches long). Starting from the layout reference line, label each point, "*A*" through "*J*". See the side view.

♦3   Divide the *bottom* horizontal edge into nine equal spaces (approximately 2²¹/₃₂-inch spaces). Label each point, "*1*" through "*9*." See the side view.

♦4   The actual *curve* is created with *straight* lines. Draw a straight line from "*B*" to "*1*", "*C*" to "*2*", "*D*" to "*3*", and so on, until you get to "*I*" to "*9*". This will form a perfect parabolic curve.

♦5   Take a compass and set it at 3 inches. With the point set on the parabolic curve, scribe a series of 3-inch arcs at intervals of about 1 inch along the curve. This will give a nice "parallel" line to the constructed curve exactly 3 inches away.

(Continued on the following three pages.)

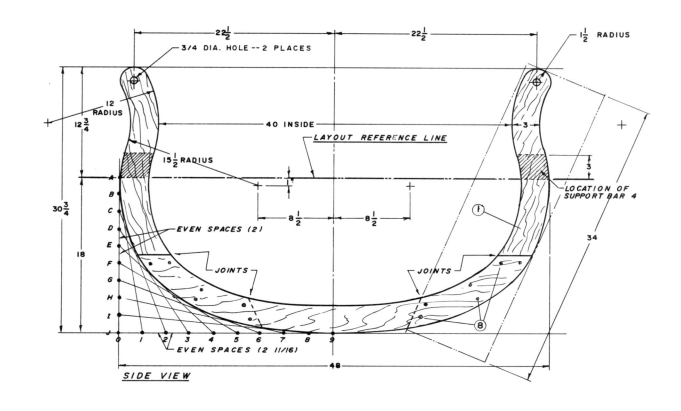

SIDE VIEW

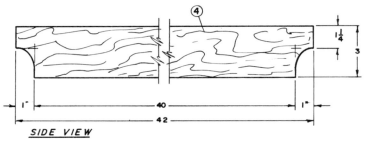

SIDE VIEW

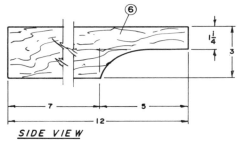

SIDE VIEW

NO.	NAME	SIZE	REQ'D.
1	ROCKER ASSEMBLY	3/4 X 10 – 8'-0" LG.	4
2	FOOT REST	3/4 X 3–14 LONG	6
3	HANDLE	3/4 DIA. – 15 LONG	2
4	SUPPORT BAR	3/4 X 3 – 50 LONG	2
5	CROSS SPACER	3/4 X 3 – 9 1/2 LONG	3
6	CENTER BRACE	3/4 X 3 – 12 LONG	2
7	SEAT	3/4 X 11–15 LONG	2
8	SCREW – FL. HD.	NO 8 – 1 3/8 LONG	46

♦6 Complete the top section of the rocker using the given dimensions and radius. This completes a full-size pattern of the left side. Refer to the exploded view. Note how the rocker, part number 1, is actually made up of six small pieces overlapped, screwed, and glued together.

♦7 Transfer the pattern to the wood, and cut out all six pieces (actually twelve counting *both* sides).

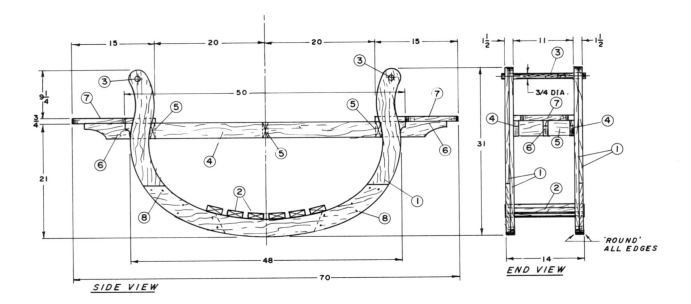

SIDE VIEW

END VIEW

'ROUND' ALL EDGES

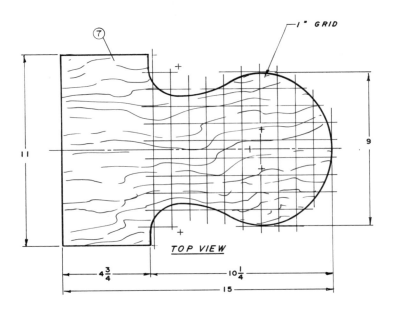

TOP VIEW

1" GRID

♦8 Glue and screw the pieces together; see the exploded view. Locate and drill the ¾-inch-diameter holes.

♦9 Sand all over. "Round" all edges—especially the bottom edge.

♦10 Make up the seats, support bars, and center braces, parts number 7, 4, and 6. Sand all over.

♦11 Cut all other pieces to size. Sand all over.

♦12 Assemble the support bars, parts number 4, to the cross spacers, parts number 5.

♦13 Add the seats, parts number 7, and center braces, parts number 6.

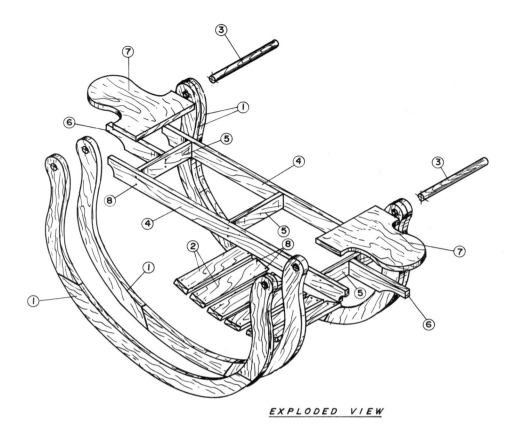

EXPLODED VIEW

♦14 Glue and nail the foot rests, parts number 2, to the rocker assembly.

♦15 Add the support bar and seat assembly.

♦16 Add the two handles, parts number 3. This completes the assembly.

♦17 Sand all over. "Round" all edges.

♦18 Finish to suit. Now comes the fun!

Metric Conversion

Inches to Millimetres and Centimetres

MM—millimetres   CM—centimetres

Inches	MM	CM	Inches	CM	Inches	CM
⅛	3	0.3	9	22.9	30	76.2
¼	6	0.6	10	25.4	31	78.7
⅜	10	1.0	11	27.9	32	81.3
½	13	1.3	12	30.5	33	83.8
⅝	16	1.6	13	33.0	34	86.4
¾	19	1.9	14	35.6	35	88.9
⅞	22	2.2	15	38.1	36	91.4
1	25	2.5	16	40.6	37	94.0
1¼	32	3.2	17	43.2	38	96.5
1½	38	3.8	18	45.7	39	99.1
1¾	44	4.4	19	48.3	40	101.6
2	51	5.1	20	50.8	41	104.1
2½	64	6.4	21	53.3	42	106.7
3	76	7.6	22	55.9	43	109.2
3½	89	8.9	23	58.4	44	111.8
4	102	10.2	24	61.0	45	114.3
4½	114	11.4	25	63.5	46	116.8
5	127	12.7	26	66.0	47	119.4
6	152	15.2	27	68.6	48	121.9
7	178	17.8	28	71.1	49	124.5
8	203	20.3	29	73.7	50	127.0

Index

Other Woodworking Books by John A. Nelson

52 Weekend Woodworking Projects   Every one of these woodworking projects can be cut out and assembled over a weekend. From folk art to heart-shaped projects, from toys and puzzles to clocks and household items—they're all quick and easy to do and require few tools. Almost all of these rewarding projects require only basic woodworking tools, so even beginners can make them easily. Accurate and numbered shop drawings, exploded diagrams, and clear, easy-to-read instructions take you step by step through each project, from selecting materials to putting on finishes. 160 pages.

52 Country Projects for the Weekend Woodworker   You can make any of these 52 appealing woodworking projects—each an exact copy of a one-of-a-kind country classic—with basic tools and methods and a minimum of space. Make a sea-horse weather vane, a horse pull toy for a little girl or boy, a Queen Anne mirror as a gift, and many more classic projects. Directions are clear and simple, with detailed exploded construction drawings to illustrate exactly how each piece is made and assembled. You'll learn which materials to select for each project, the right joinery methods, the tools you'll need, finishing hints, and a whole host of other practical workshop techniques. 160 pages.

52 Decorative Weekend Woodworking Projects   Add some variety to your weekend woodworking with these 52 unique, quick, and easy projects! From toys and games to folk-art objects, and from practical household items to country favorites, you'll find everything you could possibly ask for in this one guide! Each project comes with full-size patterns, two- and three-view drawings of front and side and top, and exploded diagrams and section views of moulding details and techniques for joining parts. Every part is numbered, so you can see exactly where each one goes. Other time-savers: a bill of materials listed in order of use, with shortcuts for making duplicate pieces and transferring patterns to wood, as well as for enlarging or reducing any project to suit your needs. 160 pages.